Retro Home

Retro

Katherine Sorrell

Home

MERRELL
LONDON · NEW YORK

Contents

Introduction

There's retro style in us all, I believe. Who doesn't love a bit of nostalgia, a dash of kitsch or some cool mid-twentieth-century styling? Taking inspiration from the past is one of the best ways to approach any decorating project, and if that means including one or two vintage pieces, so much the better, I say. And then there are those for whom a touch of retro is not nearly enough; who get their kicks from seeking out perfect retro furniture and accessories for every room in the home. That's what is so wonderful about retro style: you can take it just as far as you want. No one says you have to obey any rules, and if all-over retro is what you're after, great; if you prefer to keep it subtle, that's fine, too.

There's no doubt in my mind that introducing retro style to the home enhances it greatly, because it adds variety. A home filled entirely with brand-new high-street furnishings can easily end up being a little bland. You can't beat the character and sense of personality that come from a retro item – whether it's a lava lamp in a teenager's bedroom, a brightly coloured glass vase on the mantelpiece or a 1950s cocktail cabinet in your dining room.

Going retro is also interesting and satisfying. It is fun to set yourself a project: tracking down a matching set of teacups by the Midwinter pottery, say, or finding some really special dining chairs. It may take time and effort, some trips to second-hand shops, auction houses or specialist dealers,

Sideboards from the 1950s and 1960s can be relatively inexpensive, and are the backbone of many retro looks.

or perhaps a few hours trawling the internet, but surely that is so much more individual than simply buying the most obvious and easy thing.

Retro style can be 'green', too: reusing old furniture is terrifically environmentally friendly, and well-made pieces from the past can last for decades and longer. And going retro can be quite affordable. Needless to say, it all depends on what you buy, and iconic pieces by well-known designers tend to have correspondingly high price tags. But if you stick to choosing everyday items, and take

There's a touch of 1950s Scandinavian style to this light-filled dining area, thanks to the use of white and red, fur and natural timber.

your time to scour the less expensive outlets, from charity shops to car boot sales, you can often bag yourself a bargain.

How you use retro is, of course, entirely your choice. My personal definition of 'retro' is pretty loose, and my feeling is that retro means different things to different people and that they approach it from different viewpoints: from a vague inclination towards furnishings from the fairly recent past, to a strictly controlled selection of high-level, mid-twentieth-century modern design. The thing is, styles don't come and go in isolation:

For instant effect in any room, fill shelves with pretty retro accessories.

in real life, we take a bit of this and a bit of that; influences come from all around us. Also, styles change gradually, and certainly not according to the labels that we conveniently give them. The edges are blurred.

So definitions of styles are pretty hard to pin down. This is a good thing when you're mixing retro with pieces you already own (perhaps modern, perhaps antique) in the context of your home's architecture – which may or may not be from the same period. Work those blurry distinctions to your advantage. To my mind, there's nothing wrong with taking what you like from retro styles and mixing them up to create something that suits you and your home, even if it might make a purist scoff.

Look for interesting and attractive pieces, such as this eye-catching sideboard, wherever you go.

This book aims to give you some ideas about where to start with retro. It's not a history book or a prescriptive decorating bible; rather, it is more of a sourcebook of ideas and inspiration from which you can cherry-pick your favourite bits and gain confidence to do your own thing, learning a little along the way.

We begin with the basics in Retro Essentials: an introduction to what retro is (or can be); an overview of choosing retro styles and how to make them work in your home; how to buy, restore and care for retro furniture; and the pros and cons of reproduction pieces versus the genuine article.

The second section, Retro Styles, is a more in-depth guide to various looks, from a plain and simple, charming style that sums

Furnishings that have been well chosen for their distinctive outlines and varied textures make this retro room instantly appealing.

up a sense of pre-war nostalgia, right through to the 'pop' look of the 1960s and early 1970s. Anyone who enjoys retro furniture and accessories will find a style that's to their taste here – or certainly a host of good-looking elements that they can mix and match to their heart's content. In addition, each of the chapters in this section contains an extra or two, in the form of mini-features on key designs or designers of the times.

The next section, Case Studies, is an irresistible selection of rooms in real-life homes. From living rooms, dining rooms and kitchens to bedrooms, bathrooms and home offices, they are decorated in a wide range of appealing retro styles. Some of the rooms are luxurious and aspirational, others are budget-minded and easily achievable; some owners have used retro in a pure and all-encompassing way, while others have combined it with modern furnishings for an easy-going, contemporary look. What the rooms all have in common is the unique style that retro adds.

The book concludes with an invaluable international directory of suppliers, which will help you to source your favourite retro look, whether it is kitsch or designer, Scandi or 1960s, to supplement your hunt at charity shops, car boot sales, markets, antiques retailers and second-hand dealers. And now, armed with both information and inspiration, there's nothing stopping you: it's time to launch into retro heaven.

Retro

Essentials

What is Retro?

Don't worry about following rules: interpret retro in whatever way works best for you.

Just what is retro? That's a good question. The word 'retro' means different things to different people, and there's a fine line – and sometimes no line at all – between retro and antique, retro and kitsch, retro and vintage, retro and mid-century modern, retro and good old second-hand ... You get the picture.

'Retro' relates to, or is reminiscent of, things past, so could refer to pretty much anything that is older than about twenty-five years or so; but retro items shouldn't be confused with 'proper' antiques, which are generally accepted as having been made more than 100 years ago. Therefore, retro relates to anything from around the time of the First World War to the mid-1980s (and I'm going to discount the 1980s altogether as the decade that style forgot). Dealers in retro furnishings, however, may well have their

Despite the designer moulded plywood chair (by Norman Cherner, 1958), this kitchen has a rather basic, spare look that perfectly evokes a retro feel.

Old metal furnishings, all the nicer for showing a bit of wear and tear, give this study a fabulously vintage/industrial look.

Even though the furniture and accessories are from different periods, the overall retro look in this room is coherent and appealing. The table dates back to 1958 and the chairs are from the 1970s, while the ceramics were made in Italy between 1928 and 1954.

The white plastic seat and Eiffel Tower-like metal legs give this chair a distinctively 1950s Eames-like style.

own interpretation of what the term means, and while some may be all-inclusive as regards time frames, others may feel that retro relates only to, say, the 1950s.

It's important to remember that retro is about a lot more than just a date. It is also the evocation, either subtle or strong, of a certain era, and perhaps of a certain place, too: an American diner, for example, or a Scandinavian designer home. Retro inevitably induces strong feelings, whether of nostalgia, glamour, eccentricity, humour or sophistication. As we shall see in later chapters, retro can be polished and poised, or quirky and fun; it can be chic and minimal, or it can be bold and bright. What's certain is that retro, however you interpret the term, has heaps of character and a unique sense of style.

Opposite: The juxtaposition of period architectural details and retro furniture can be dramatic and impressive.

Choosing a Style

How do you live? What do you love?
With retro, it's all a question of
personal taste.

The colours, shapes and patterns of these fabulous ceramics are very evocative of the 1950s. They would be perfect in any retro scheme.

Which retro are you? There's a world of difference between a retro look that evokes a pastel world of floral eiderdowns (page 42), and one that encompasses the bold colours and 'far-out' plastic shapes of the 1960s (page 114). And while one fan of retro may have a penchant for the blonde wood of Scandinavian Sleek (page 66), another may prefer the poodles and flying ducks of the kitsch 1950s (page 90). Fortunately, there are no hard and fast rules, and you're free to choose whichever retro style suits you – or even a mix of them.

A good way to start is by thinking about the architecture of your home. On a practical level, low, lean, slender furniture will work best in a small apartment, while big, bold pieces will be better off in a high-ceilinged, larger space. Think about the furniture you possess. If all your things are pretty and floral,

Rounded squares and vivid orange are straight out of the fab and funky 1960s.

then it makes sense to go towards a Nostalgic retro look rather than a wham-bam bold style; if you have already collected a few special designer pieces, then you will want to build on what you've got.

Having said that, your personal preferences will ultimately be the most important factor when choosing a retro style: aim to develop your sense of decorative likes and dislikes by looking around you and taking inspiration from everything you can. Books and magazines are obvious ports of call, but so are friends' houses, hotels, shops, restaurants, the natural world, films, paint charts, television shows – you name it, it can all help. You may want to put together a scrapbook of ideas: cuttings from magazines; swatches of fabric, wallpaper and flooring; brushes of favourite paint colours. If authenticity important to you, learn about your favourite stylistic eras, key designers and important manufacturers. Ultimately, however, you can research the history of a style as much or as little as you like, but it all comes down to what you like, what you love, and what you can't live without.

A black moulded-plastic chair by Verner Panton (see page 119) and an arching metal lamp look marvellous set against the patina of an old wooden table.

Put together a traditional metal bedstead, a wooden-cased clock, an old-fashioned desk lamp and a vintage flag, and you've got instant nostalgic style.

Making it Work

Clever ideas and practical advice
to help to ensure retro success.

A little retro can go a long way, especially in
a modern home: it can be fabulous, or it can
be overwhelming. In a period property, retro
pieces can provide a wonderful contrast
to the architecture, but there is also the
potential for disastrous conflict. So just how
do you make retro style work for you?

Introducing a retro flavour to your home by
displaying key pieces that complement your
existing furnishings is the simplest strategy,
and adds interest quickly, easily and without
risk; or you can go all out and create a totally
retro room, a passionate evocation of all-
encompassing style. If the latter approach
interests you, do your research and ensure that
your furnishings all fit in with the look; you'll
probably need to be patient while you wait
for the right pieces to turn up in auctions or
specialist shops. Either way, use the tips and
tricks on page 23 to help in your search.

The low, lean, boxy shapes
of these items of furniture
are redolent of the 1950s,
even though they are modern.
The old-fashioned telephone
is a nice touch.

Opposite: Stretch a length of vintage fabric over a large artist's canvas and you've got an instant, eye-catching wall hanging.

Collect old vases from markets and second-hand shops. Look for interesting shapes and coordinating colours, then put them together as a display.

Furniture with spindly legs always looks a little bit 1950s, even when it is contemporary.

Tips and Tricks

◉ Choose colours with care. Certain palettes typify individual retro styles: pale, pretty pastels for Nostalgic, for example, or sunshine-yellow, sherbet-pink and tangerine for the 1950s. Select the right colours for your retro look and they will set the scene, unify disparate elements, disguise flaws and highlight your room's most desirable features.

◉ Pick your patterns wisely. For that Nostalgic retro look, you'd want to opt for tiny flowers and simple ticking stripes, while for 1950s kitsch it would be abstract geometrics, satellites, cowboys or poodles.

◉ Consider size, scale and overall form. Of course your furniture should suit the size of the room but, more subliminally, it helps if your pieces share an aesthetic that unifies them visually. In a sleek and streamlined Luxe Moderne room, for example, an overstuffed sofa would stand out like a sore thumb.

◉ And a final tip: if in doubt, take it out. Clutter just confuses, whereas if you develop a 'less is more' attitude for your rooms, your retro choices will have greater impact and look more beautiful.

Buying Retro

Where to source those perfect pieces, at all budgets.

When you shop on the high street, provided your pockets are deep enough, you can get almost anything you like in an instant. Buying retro for your home, however, involves more patience, thought and effort. Retro furnishings could turn up anywhere, from second-hand shops to high-end dealers, and from auction houses to flea markets, so it helps to start by focusing on exactly what you're looking for. If you are keen simply to add a little decorative flair, it won't be a problem to pick up one or two good-looking items plus the odd accessory. But if you're serious about authenticity and creating an accurate overall look, you'll need to research your chosen era, designers and makers, and to select your sources with care.

First, the free stuff: skip-dipping and visiting free-exchange internet groups, such as Freecycle, can result in some surprisingly

Kitsch ornaments: there is no middle way, you either love them or hate them. It is up to you whether you include them in your scheme.

Piles of colour-coded vintage fabric are decorative accessories in themselves, while the evocative typography and illustrations on vintage tins and boxes add to the overall effect.

When you come across a one-off piece that you fall in love with straight away, snap it up. You'll always regret it if you don't.

interesting – although probably not valuable – finds, especially if you're a dab hand at mending or 'upcycling'. Don't take anything out of a skip without asking permission first, however, and I feel that if you're given something on Freecycle it's a good idea to give something away in return (it's a karma thing).

Then there are car boot sales and garage sales, junk shops and salvage yards. You never know when you might be passing one of these potential treasure troves, so my best advice is always to have a tape measure about your person, as well as a list of vital dimensions (for example, 'sofa no wider than xx or it won't fit through the front hall'). Auctions, both online and real-life, are brilliant places in which to find retro furniture and accessories, at all ends of the scale, from the finest designer chair to a cracked china cup, but take care not to get carried away and go over-budget.

And finally, antiques shops and specialist dealers are ideal sources of classy pieces, although it's never a good idea to buy something purely because you think it will increase in value. Ask lots of questions; a good dealer will not mind at all. And, when you've settled on your must-have purchase, make the polite request: 'What's your best price?' There may be a margin for civilized negotiation, turning your ideal retro piece into an affordable, as well as a desirable, option.

If you're going retro, you'll have to train yourself to be a hunter-gatherer, looking out for furniture and accessories everywhere you go.

Repro Retro Versus the Real Deal

Buying repro can be a bit of
a minefield, so make sure you
know what you're getting.

As well as 'real' retro – original pieces that have survived through the years – it is also possible to buy reissued and reproduction retro pieces. When a designer piece is reissued by its licensed manufacturer, it will usually be made with the same materials (subject to twenty-first-century suitability) and to the same specifications as the original; you are guaranteed a brand-new piece that's of the highest quality, with no compromise on authenticity of design.

If you like your retro look unworn and undamaged, reissues are great, but they come at a price. 'Reproduction', on the other hand, could mean anything: while some manufacturers work to the highest standards, using appropriate materials and (subject to copyright) authentic designs, others cut corners, and, over time, that will show. Reproduction pieces are cheaper – sometimes a great deal

You may need to save for some time to buy a lounger and ottoman designed by Charles and Ray Eames (see page 107), whether original 1950s or reissue. Retro lovers will consider it well worth the effort, however.

Even modern furniture can offer a fresh take on old themes: lean upholstery, shagpile carpet and curvy ceramics, for example, are all both old and new.

mple soft furnishings KATRIN CARGILL

In this relaxed living room, a classic Tulip side table (designed by Eero Saarinen in the 1950s) sits happily among both new and old furnishings.

Right: This fabulous retro look could be achieved relatively easily, whatever your budget (although if you want a genuine Tulip table, bear in mind that it's an iconic design and carries a correspondingly high price tag).

Below: It is possible to buy new radios that have a very similar style to this lovely vintage Bush model.

cheaper – than reissues, but prices can vary wildly. It's tempting to say that you get what you pay for, but rip-offs can be rife in this market, unfortunately.

Some people feel that they should not buy reproduction for moral reasons; others just cannot otherwise afford the look they want on their budget. It's a grey area, but what is certain is that, when buying retro, you must make sure that you absolutely know what you are getting.

If you are tempted by something because it's attractive and suits your home, and you feel that authenticity, quality or durability are not relevant, you may decide that a cheap reproduction piece is a bargain and just right for you, but otherwise you'll want to avoid being sold a fake that you believed to be an original. This applies particularly when buying online, where descriptions can be inaccurate and photographs are not always clear. But even when buying in person, it's worth checking. If you've done your research you'll know if there should be a maker's mark hidden underneath, or a tell-tale design sign that would let you know you're getting the real deal. Never be afraid to ask the seller lots of questions, and follow your instincts as to whether or not he or she is trustworthy. As is the case with so many other things, remember: with retro, it's buyer beware.

Restoration, Restoration, Restoration

Some repairs are easy; others require an expert. But always take care if your piece is rare or valuable.

You may find retro furnishings for sale in pristine condition, but it is more likely that they will be – unsurprisingly, considering their age – a touch battered round the edges. Only you can decide just what level of wear and tear you are prepared to accept, but it goes without saying that the more worn-out the piece, the cheaper it should be; and if something is badly damaged you may want to pass it over entirely.

For a DIY enthusiast, a chair with a wobbly leg may not be a problem. You may even be prepared to go on a course so as to learn a new skill, such as carpentry, upholstery or sewing. But even the most competent layperson won't have the equipment or expertise to do everything: working with metal or old plastics, for example, could prove tricky, and electrical rewiring should be tackled only by a certified electrician.

Got a genuine 1950s Eames rocking chair in need of restoration? Take it to an expert for assessment, as a poor repair may decrease its value.

The boot's on the other leg: an ingenious and original solution for a problem table.

Some faults are more of a problem than others, of course, and if you require of your piece only that it look decorative, it might not matter if it's a little fragile. If, on the other hand, you want a piece that withstands the rigours of daily use, then before you buy you must either ensure that you are able to restore it fully yourself or factor in the cost of employing someone else to do so.

There is also the question of whether or not you should ever alter a valuable or rare retro piece, even to repair it. As a general rule, apply minimal intervention in bringing your retro furnishings up to scratch, using materials and techniques as close to the original as possible, and if you have any doubt as to whether what you plan to do is appropriate, always seek expert advice.

This pretty chest of drawers has been well restored to pristine condition.

This beautiful mint-and-cream vintage cabinet, with its glass panels engraved in an Art Deco style, is just the sort of thing that would require expert attention, should it ever need repair.

Caring for Retro Furniture

However robust your retro piece,
it will benefit from a little love
and attention.

All but the most delicate of retro furnishings will give you years of trouble-free life, but, just to make sure, it's worth being aware of some general rules about how best to care for them. For example, direct sunlight makes colours fade and can, in the long run, cause damage to both wood and textiles. Changes in humidity can cause wood to warp and split, so it's best to avoid placing precious pieces near fires, radiators or air-conditioning vents, or in bathrooms; also, do not store them in basements or lofts. And in certain conditions, such as damp, organic materials, including wood, horsehair and leather, can become infested with beetles or other insects. Look for tiny exit holes – you'll know if they're active because they'll contain a fine, sawdust-like material – and, if necessary, have the piece fumigated by a specialist.

Left and opposite: Having checked old wooden furniture for insect activity, you must gently dust and clean it regularly. A light wax once a year or so can also be beneficial.

Such delicate surfaces as velvet and animal skin need special care. A cowhide rug, for example, should be shaken or gently vacuumed to remove dust, and wiped in the direction of the hair with a damp cloth, using a mild soapy solution.

Regular dusting and cleaning are a good idea. Use a soft cotton cloth or artist's brush, slightly dampened if dirt is stubborn, but never anything abrasive. To care for leather furniture, vacuum it gently and wipe it with a damp cloth; use specialist products, if necessary, to polish and remove stains. For wooden pieces, avoid oils and sprays, as they tend to build up into a sticky coating that can actually attract more dirt; it's better just to apply wax once a year and polish.

As for moving old furniture, first take off shelves and drawers, and secure doors (assuming they can't be removed easily) with a soft strap. Lift the piece, don't drag it; and remember that tops and arms may be accidentally pulled from bases unless you lift the piece by its main frame or from under the seat. Treat your furniture with respect: don't lean back on two legs of a chair, or open drawers by pulling on one handle when there are two. Protect it from knocks, scratches and spills, and your piece should last forever and become a treasured retro antique.

Keep retro furniture in sparkling condition by cleaning it regularly, using products recommended by your supplier.

Retro

Styles

Look Back in Nostalgia

Step back into a world that is simple and pretty, evoking a pleasurable, timeless charm.

A Nostalgic retro style has enduring appeal. It's gentle and charming, unassuming and unfussy, achievable without difficulty and easy on the eye. This is a look that is probably more about a pleasurable and pretty-much imaginary notion of days gone by than about any historical reality, but I see no harm in that. It encompasses plain and simple furniture (possibly a little country-style, but definitely not twee), ticking stripes and delicate florals, handmade pieces and pale paint colours. If you can add a little Fair Isle knitting, some heavy woollen blankets and a dresser chock-full of pretty crockery, so much the better.

The building blocks of the Nostalgic style are polished or painted wooden floorboards (with rugs wherever necessary), unfussy floor tiles or neutral-coloured wool carpets. Walls might be painted just slightly off-white (brilliant white was not available until after

Simple touches, such as a patterned rug and a dressing gown, can transform an otherwise plain room cheaply and easily.

Use paint to freshen up an old chair. This soft blue is terrific, and prettily echoes the colour in the portrait above.

the Second World War) or, for interest, you could go for wallpaper featuring rosebuds, peonies or hydrangeas – either tiny, spriggy florals or blowsy blooms – in fresh and pastel colours. Tongue-and-groove panelling, or bevel-edged tiles laid in a brick-bond pattern, are also suitably traditional finishes for walls, particularly in bathrooms and kitchens.

Nostalgic retro isn't a style that harks back very far in time: no dark, heavy Victorian oak or pine furniture, and no Georgian mahogany pieces – they're proper antiques and just not right for this look. But neither does it include

Inexpensive furniture can work brilliantly for the Nostalgic look, and sometimes it's a case of the more battered it is, the better.

This lovely display combines an 'inspiration wall' with teapots and a watering can, which makes a charming informal vase.

Planked doors, an old-fashioned phone, a painting of flying ducks and a wooden lamp give this study area a relaxed and Nostalgic feel.

Below: Scouring markets, sales and antiques shops for just the right accessories, such as this patterned butter dish, can be great fun.

look-at-me, glossy twentieth-century designer pieces. The style is about sturdy, useful, timeless chairs, tables, dressers, sideboards, beds, chests and wardrobes, in bare wood or painted white, cream or a pale pastel (the last being a modern take on the look); it also takes in a little bit of shabby chic. Perfection isn't important — in fact, you should positively avoid it. This is a style where knocked-about corners and faded colours enhance the effect rather than detract from it.

Equally, it doesn't matter if the furniture is mismatched, provided it follows the overall aesthetic. Take a set of simple wooden dining chairs, for example: so long as they fit around your table, there is no harm if they're slightly different in construction from one another, or a little distressed. You could always give them a lick of paint to freshen them up and unify the look. Sofas and armchairs should be

The Nostalgic look is a natural choice if you have a framework of aged floorboards and bare bricks to paint, and — the *pièce de résistance* — an old range cooker.

Patchwork Quilts

Whether traditional or modern in style, a patchwork quilt is always a wonderful addition to a Nostalgic bedroom.

Patchwork quilts reached the peak of their popularity in Great Britain and North America in the nineteenth century, but their rich history goes back thousands of years. Medieval European quilting was used, as it is today, mostly for bedcovers. Silk or taffeta quilts, embroidered with metallic thread, were made by professionals for noble families, while the less well-off used any scraps of fabric, pieced together and layered with worn wool.

When textile production in the United Kingdom expanded from the 1760s, patchworking developed rapidly. Genteel ladies passed their time creating fine mosaic or embroidered coverlets, while rural and provincial communities made whole-cloth

or 'medallion' quilts (with a large central motif, and often having multiple borders), stitched with regionally typical designs. Towards the end of the nineteenth century the arrival of the domestic sewing machine further fuelled the popularity of patchwork. 'Strippy' quilts (made from strips rather than squares) were made mainly in north-east England; elsewhere, the Victorian and early twentieth-century craze was for hexagonal patchwork, while American quilters were known for their exuberant 'block' quilts, in which patches are joined together to make a design, such as a star. Home-made quilts were out of fashion by the middle of the twentieth century, but they're back with a vengeance now and, whether old or new, are perfect for a Nostalgic retro look.

Ercol

Ercol's sleek, spare furniture is a British classic, perfect for a retro-style home. The company (initially called Furniture Industries) was estabished in 1920 by Lucian Ercolani (1888–1976) in High Wycombe, Buckinghamshire, which at the time was the furniture-making capital of England. Ercolani's aim was to produce high-quality, classic furniture with a modern twist, and his company went from strength to strength. In 1944 he was contracted by the British government to produce 10,000 low-cost chairs; his fresh and simple Windsor chair, for which he used steam-bent English elm, not often used in furniture-making, was attractive, lightweight and affordable, and it became a huge hit. At the 1951 Festival of Britain (see page 81), Ercol furniture was displayed as an example of the very latest fashion. Other Ercol classics to look out for include the 1950s Quaker chair (below), the nest of 'pebble' tables (1956), the Stacking chair (1957), the Butterfly chair (1958) and the Studio couch (late 1950s), all good-looking, comfortable and uniquely redolent of clean-lined mid-century style.

Ercol's Quaker chair, designed by Lucian Ercolani in the 1950s, is a timeless classic that works in both modern and traditional rooms.

squashy, rather than sleek and streamlined or frilly and flouncy, and a patch or two is fine. This is a look that's perfect for the eco-aware and budget-conscious among us: no need to throw old furniture away, simply give it a new life in your eclectic retro home.

Choose just the right fabric, and getting the Nostalgic look will be effortless. Think linen and lace, ticking and tweed, distressed leather, soft mohair and heavy wool. Plains, stripes and faded florals are ideal, as are the classic paisleys of old-fashioned Liberty prints. Have you picked up some vintage linen

In a retro Nostalgic room you can't go wrong with a spot of pink among natural timber and vintage accessories.

Painted wooden cabinets, floral curtains and a floor laid with plain square tiles add up to a room that is both attractive and functional.

curtains at a French flea market? Make a loose cover for a small sofa. You've got an old Welsh blanket with a threadbare corner? Fold it and drape it over the back of an armchair.

Don't forget window treatments: simple gathered curtains, and Roman and roller blinds, can all be made from vintage fabric (provided it is neither too heavy nor too light). And if you're handy with a needle, use up the leftovers by running up some cushion covers. The fabrics don't have to match, but take care that your colours and patterns are complementary rather than clashing. In the bedroom, go for a super-cosy look with piles of patchwork quilts and satin eiderdowns, and add some knitting and crochet (granny squares in mad colours are great) for delightful textural effect.

The finishing touches make or break any retro style and so, for a nicely Nostalgic look, collect an assortment of pastel-coloured ceramics or creamware, melamine, pressed glass and any other bits and pieces that you think complement them; it could be gadgets (there are some fab and functional retro-style items of kitchen kit around, and they look perfect with a retro-style fridge): a Bakelite phone or a soda siphon, perhaps. At hardly any expense you could mix in some modern-day reproduction items, such as floral-printed or polka-dot mugs, a vase or a stack of biscuit tins. Make a feature of these accessories as individual items or, better still, for marvellous,

Nothing could be cosier than a mix of cream paintwork, floral eiderdowns, a pretty mirror and a Lloyd Loom chair. Fresh flowers in the same colour tones add a finishing touch.

massed effect, group them on a kitchen shelf, sideboard or dresser (possibly lined at the back with some colourful wallpaper). In the kitchen you could also go to town with Nostalgic tea towels and oven gloves, aprons and storage jars, while bathrooms can be beautified with lace- or floral-edged towels and yet more pretty storage.

Lastly, light up your life with some Nostalgic retro-style light fittings. These could range from a simple, droplet-style chandelier to a functional Anglepoise lamp, and from a rise-and-fall ceramic pendant to a frilly-edged lampshade on a wooden base. The aim is to achieve a look of eclectic individuality that is not show-offy or overly sophisticated, kitsch or clever. Put it all together, and what is the result? Yesterday's treasures, beautifully aged or subtly re-created in modern form, become today's evocative pleasures.

For the Nostalgic look, choose free-standing furniture rather than built-in. It often has more character.

Old-fashioned children's toys can be fantastic collector's items, and look wonderful displayed on a shelf.

Luxe Moderne

A sophisticated look that is at once subtle and striking, this style is as grown-up and glamorous as it comes.

A juxtaposition of glossy black and pearly pastels is very Luxe, whether as an overall scheme or an interesting detail.

Not all retro styles give off a vibe of luxurious living; most, in fact, steer more towards frugality, frivolity, kitsch or cool. One of the exceptions is Luxe Moderne, which takes its inspiration from two styles that developed in Europe and the United States in the 1920s and 1930s, and combines the opulent good looks of Art Deco with Modernism's emphasis on space, light and sleek, flowing lines. We're talking concrete, steel and glass (just as modern today as they were nearly a century ago), plus such tactile materials as leather, silk and velvet, and eye-catching touches, such as animal prints, vivid colours or stylized ziggurat or sunray patterns. Picture yourself drinking cocktails or dancing the Charleston in the ballroom of Claridge's, and you're already halfway there.

The starting point is easy: plain walls — pale to maximize the sense of space, or darker for dramatic impact — and plain flooring; you

Black always makes a statement when it's the dominant colour in a scheme. Good natural light is essential to ensure that the room does not feel oppressive.

might choose polished wooden boards or parquet, stone, lino or wall-to-wall carpet. Add rugs with bold, abstract geometric patterns, or even a fake animal skin or two. As for colours, pure Modernists would want to stick to a palette of white, black, grey and taupe (grey with a tinge of brown), perhaps with one or two primary colours in the style of the Bauhaus school of the 1920s and accessorized with chrome. For a Deco atmosphere, you could include such interesting shades as eau de Nil (a pale green), peach, lime-green, beige, orange and mauve.

To get the Deco style, look for bold pieces with sweeping, curved lines, as in the armchair above. Lighting should be elegant and luxurious, as seen in the lamp pictured right.

A monochrome palette is ultra-sophisticated. Here, a glamorous mix of velvet, satin and glass offers textural interest.

Le Corbusier

Born Charles Edouard Jeanneret in Switzerland, Le Corbusier (1887–1965) was a pioneer of modern design: a painter, writer, furniture designer, town planner and architect whose ideas were to become the bedrock of twentieth-century style.

Le Corbusier made his name at the Paris Exposition Internationale des Arts Décoratifs et Industriels of 1925 with an all-white pavilion called l'Esprit Nouveau ('the new spirit'). Its unusual style (later dubbed Modernist), which was typified by the use of concrete and glass, tubular steel, plain surfaces and a lack of ornamentation, caused a scandal.

Le Corbusier also collaborated with his cousin Pierre Jeanneret and the architect Charlotte Perriand on furniture designs, and some of these pieces have become modern classics, including the B306 chaise longue of 1928 (below and opposite, top) and the chromed tubular-steel Grand Confort chair and sofa, also of 1928 (shown opposite, bottom).

Le Corbusier's bent tubular steel and leather B306 chaise longue, launched in 1928, is a classic of the period.

The B306 chaise longue adds instant 1920s style to a high-ceilinged, open-plan space.

Furniture has to be streamlined, chic and sleek. Modernism's guiding principle was that form should follow function – an object's overall look should result from the way in which it actually works, and not feature frills and fancies that have been added to make it superficially attractive. Therefore, avoid anything that is unnecessarily decorative, over-padded, garishly patterned or just madly exuberant. Instead, think spare, efficient, light and durable, in such 'industrial' materials as tubular steel, plywood, glass, leather and chrome. That said, for a bit of Deco dash, there is a case to be made for the addition of the occasional exotic finish – a mahogany sideboard, lacquer cabinet or tortoiseshell cigar case, say – or such inlays as mother-of-pearl or shagreen (sharkskin or untanned leather).

Modernist furnishings are not so very far from what we're all used to today: bent-ply stools and cantilevered chairs, modular and built-in pieces. Art Deco furniture, however, typically tends to be fairly solid in style, low and with rounded corners. A little goes a long way. If in doubt, opt for something plain and simple, and add a statement piece or

The blocky form of the Grand Confort club chair, designed in 1928 by Le Corbusier, Charlotte Perriand and Pierre Jeanneret, contrasts with the fluid shapes of the equally iconic Butterfly Stool (*c.* 1955) by the Japanese–American designer Sori Yanagi.

Right and below, right: To get the Luxe Moderne look, choose such materials as metallics, mirror, velvet and suede, and team them with a monochromatic background.

An Art Deco leather armchair is the focal point in the corner of this gold-wallpapered room.

In a Luxe scheme, aim for sophisticated colours plus a dash of drama, sleek contours and an overall air of luxury.

two, such as a mirrored dressing table or a chrome-and-glass drinks trolley (complete with cocktail shaker and Martini glasses).

When choosing upholstery, it is best to opt for black or brown leather or a plain, hard-wearing fabric, such as canvas or chenille, and windows should also be understated: simple, gathered curtains in a plain fabric, or a Roman, roller or Venetian blind. In the bedroom, it's easy to achieve a Luxe Moderne look: plain and neutral bedlinen (dare you go for oyster-coloured silk sheets?), plus a silk eiderdown and perhaps velvet or

silk cushions, or a fake-fur throw or a tasselled shawl. For fabric in general, leather, suede, silk, satin, canvas, cotton, velvet, chenille and moquette (a thick pile fabric) are all suitable; if you have a plain sofa, you could add cushions with patterns that are redolent of the period: sunrays, lightning flashes, zigzags, ziggurats, chevrons, shells, fans and stylized flowers. Then add silk tassels or fringing for extra effect.

Nothing says glamour like an all-out glamourpuss bathroom, and for the Luxe Moderne style it's a solid yet elegant backdrop of black and white tiles, or maybe minty green,

The technology that digitally printed these wall tiles and the oversized image is modern, but the glossy, opulent effect is just right for the Luxe Moderne look.

plus chunky white sanitaryware with bevelled edges and hexagonal taps. A claw-foot bath is a must, and you should include lots of chrome and mirror for a shiny, high-end feel.

Lighting adds enormously to a sense of style, and you can get away with taking a few liberties with the overall design provided you get your lights right. For a Luxe Moderne look, use concealed lighting (it was just coming in as *the* thing in designer pads of the time) or minimalist spotlights to provide all-purpose light, and add typically 1920s and 1930s fittings. No-nonsense Anglepoise lamps

Go for glamour in the bathroom; here it is achieved by a high-end combination of marble and beaten metal, with coordinating accessories.

are perfect, as are column-shaped chrome or
glass table lamps, marbled glass bowls (hung
from the ceiling by three chains) and shell- or
fan-shaped wall lights. For Deco decadence,
you can't go wrong if you opt for a lamp with
a statuette base (for example, a sunray, leaping
gazelle, female figure or borzoi dog), while
shades could be deeply tasselled silk or, for
a less-is-more approach, plain canvas or card.

All this brings us to that most enjoyable
area, in which impact is easy to achieve:
accessories. Framed prints of work by artists
of the period are an obvious choice, as are

A pair of tall table lamps
creates a dramatic display.
The console table and
suede cube are suitably
sophisticated for this look.

You can't go wrong with an exotic animal print in a Luxe room, although it is best used with subtlety, as above.

black-and-white photographs of iconic Deco or Modernist buildings. Alternatively, a vintage travel poster would really set the tone. A well-placed mirror is as good as a work of art, and, for impact, you could even fill a whole wall with mirrors; choose examples with bevelled edges and fanned outlines.

And then there are the many finishing touches that are quintessentially Deco in style, from a bronze ornament or a chrome clock to a Bakelite radio with sunrise motif or a silvered bedroom dressing-table set (hairbrush, comb, hand mirror, powder puff

Below: Black-and-white stripes provide an eye-catching backdrop for this sunburst clock.

It is possible to create a fabulous Luxe effect simply by repainting an old piece of wooden furniture. This acid-yellow is unusual but dramatic, and works brilliantly.

and so on). Colourful ceramics by Clarice Cliff or Susie Cooper, two of the most important British Art Deco ceramics designers, are examplars of the style.

Art Deco accessories are easy to come by at all price levels, at all sorts of places ranging from junk shops to the grandest auction house. Don't display too many, however. One or two in each room will set the tone without going over the top, because, overall, this is a look that's cool, clean and uncluttered, a clever combination of the restrained and the striking; it is grown-up, glam and utterly gorgeous.

Scandı Sleek

This good-looking retro style combines functionality and comfort, and works perfectly in a contemporary home.

It may be a retro style, but Scandi Sleek is as modern as they come. It's a look that takes open-plan, light and airy spaces and fills them with comfortable, good-looking furnishings. It's for people who want their homes to be warm and cosy in winter, and fresh and light in summer; who love pales and neutrals, natural wood, cast-iron stoves, curvy, ergonomic furniture, tactile accessories and bright splashes of gorgeous colour. Yet despite its bang-up-to-date feel, the look is rooted in European Modernism of the 1930s, from which it gradually evolved into its own distinctive

The typical Scandi look relies on a light and airy environment, blonde wood, pale colours and natural materials.

Alvar Aalto designed his three-legged birch stool in 1932–33, using a unique wood-bending technology. In 1935 he went on to use the L-shaped leg design in similar tables.

floor covering. Boards can be left as they come, or be stained, waxed, oiled, varnished or limewashed to bring out the grain and patina of the wood.

For cosy-toe comfort, throw down a sheepskin rug or two, or perhaps a woven rug in narrow stripes or broad blocks of bold colour. After all, Scandi Sleek is not just about pale and airy interiors; accents of vivid colour can provide a warming counterpoint, particularly a fab bright red. Pattern, too, is something that can be introduced judiciously, as a localized highlight rather

Left: Nubbly fabrics are soft and cosy, even in a light, bright room.

Below: A wood-burning stove will always be the focal point of a living room.

style – softer, more accessible, very human – that reached its height in Scandinavian design of the 1950s and 1960s.

Scandi Sleek is a look that is wonderfully easy to live with. For a start, the background colour palette is utterly simple: white, off-whites and natural neutrals, pale colours designed to reflect light around the home. And then there's timber, a pre-eminent feature of Scandinavian style, hard-wearing, practical and good-looking. Pale and unpainted timber is sometimes used for cladding walls, but more often appears as a beautiful, natural

than an all-round feature. Checks and stripes are perfect, or look for oversized, splashy designs in the Marimekko style (see page 71). Another lovely choice would be nature-inspired patterns by the Austrian-born architect, designer and artist Josef Frank, who emigrated to Sweden in 1933 and began working for the Stockholm interior-design company Svenskt Tenn the following year. His bold yet elegant work is unique and highly appealing.

In rooms that are, on the whole, relatively plain, any pattern naturally comes to the fore. But the plainer the room, the more important

Left, top and bottom, and below: The ingredients of a successful Scandi scheme include golden timber floors, sleek and minimalist furniture, plenty of glass, and the overall use of pale colours with the occasional splash of a more vivid shade.

The Wishbone chair – also
known as the Y chair or the
CH24 – was designed by
the Danish furniture designer
Hans Wegner in 1949 and
produced from 1950.

the part played by texture. For Scandi Sleek
fabrics, natural is the key, so when making
your choices aim for simple upholstery,
window treatments, bedlinen and table linens,
in fabrics that have subtle and attractive
variations in texture: crisp linen, soft cotton,
warm wool, floaty muslin, fluffy sheepskin
and so on. Avoid harsh, chemical-dye colours
in favour of undyed fabrics or neutral shades.

If the characteristics of Scandinavian
mid-century furniture could be summed up
in a few words, these would be 'simple',
'sculptural' and 'comfortable'. Scandinavian
designers took Modernism as a starting point,
then developed a style that was all their own,
centring on lightweight, moulded designs, often
in blonde wood, that were bent to the human
form and were, in their spare simplicity,
hugely comfortable as well as practical.

The roll-call of famous designers includes
Alvar Aalto from Finland and the Danes
Arne Jacobsen (see page 72), Finn Juhl, Poul
Kjaerholm, Kaare Klint and Hans Wegner.
Many of their designs have become classics;
indeed, some are so familiar to us that it is
hard to imagine how groundbreaking they
were when first produced. The simple
addition of an individual chair – Jacobsen's
Ant (1952; see page 118) or Egg (1958; see
page 72), or Wegner's Ox (1960) or Wishbone
(opposite), produced from 1950 by the Danish
company Carl Hansen & Co – would provide
an interior with a dramatic focal point, not

Marimekko

Europe was ready for some colour after the Second World War,
and colour was exactly what the Finnish textile and clothing
company Marimekko provided. Set up in 1951 by the husband-
and-wife team of Viljo and Armi Ratia, Marimekko (an anagram
of Armi's name and *mekko*, the Finnish word for 'dress') aimed
to create bold new patterns, and Armi (1912–1979), who was the
creative force, hired young designers to do so – her one proviso
being that she didn't want florals.

In 1964, however, Marimekko designer Maija Isola (1927–
2001) decided to ignore Armi's decree and designed an entire
collection of floral patterns, one of them being Unikko (the
famous bright, splashy poppies, shown below), which has been
a bestseller ever since. Marimekko was in the vanguard of the
mid-century lifestyle revolution, reflecting core Scandinavian
design values: simplicity, practicality, ease and comfort.

Arne Jacobsen

The Danish master of architecture and design originally trained as a bricklayer before studying architecture at the Academy of Arts, Copenhagen. Arne Jacobsen (1902–1971) became highly influenced by the Modernist aesthetic after first seeing the work of the Swiss architect Le Corbusier (see page 58) in Paris in 1925; later, however, his work became softer and more organic, and in the 1950s he began to experiment with furniture, especially using moulded plywood. In 1952 came the Ant chair (see page 118),

The Swan chair (shown in white) and the Egg (in black) combine Arne Jacobsen's Modernist ideal of pared-down, simple forms with a typically Scandinavian naturalism.

followed by the Series 7 range in 1955 and the Egg (left) and Swan (above) in 1958, and they have all been among the world's bestselling modern chairs ever since.

But it doesn't stop there: apart from his noteworthy buildings, including Copenhagen's SAS Royal Hotel (1960) and Danish National Bank (completed in the late 1970s by former employees of Jacobsen), and St Catherine's College, Oxford (1966), Jacobsen also designed lights, cutlery, textiles, glassware, candlesticks, salt and pepper shakers, taps, coffee pots and even an iconic door handle. He was truly a multi-talented design hero.

to mention a tremendous kick of Scandi retro style. Depending on your budget, look for original pieces (usually at the better dealers or auction houses), genuine reproductions or pieces made 'in the style of' – these last will be cheaper, but not necessarily as good. If your budget won't stretch to designer pieces, however, there are still plenty of options using less expensive furniture. To create this overall look, simply choose furniture with curved, organic shapes, flowing lines and slender, tapered legs, made in pale woods and with minimal upholstery.

Mid-century furniture generally has splayed legs and sleek outlines. What is noticeable about Scandinavian design, in particular, is a love of natural materials and organic forms, as seen in the chairs by Hans Wegner (above; see also photograph on page 70).

The Random light by the designer Bertjan Pot was launched by the Dutch design firm Moooi in 2002. It is simple, ethereal and slightly magical.

While Scandinavian furniture designers were key players in developing the modern look of the middle of the twentieth century, lighting designers also contributed hugely. Poul Henningsen is the name that springs most obviously to mind. The Dane's PH lamp (1925) and PH Artichoke (1958; see page 76), in which overlapping leaf-like shapes filter and disseminate light gently but efficiently, pioneered a look that many others followed. This is a style that's been copied over and over again; if you can't afford the real thing, choose either reproductions or just simple,

Flowing forms unify a huge white pendant light, a wave-like dining table and a set of Panton plastic chairs, designed by Verner Panton in 1967.

This bright and breezy dining area features a striking group of mismatched chairs. The lamp is Poul Henningsen's PH50, of 1958.

leaf-like pendants in white plastic or glass. Alternatively, go for typically 1950s-style table, wall, floor or pendant lamps; as always with Scandi style, the look must be understated to be successful: select slender, delicate, tapering lamps, in white or clear materials. Also effective are intricate folded-paper lights as seen in the amazing examples made by the Danish company Le Klint, founded in Copenhagen in 1943 and still going strong.

Scandi retro accessorizing is fun, sometimes inexpensive and always full of impact, especially when individual pieces are beautifully designed and well made – as Scandinavian accessories inevitably are. Mid-century Scandinavian designers were particularly good at glassware, silverware and quirky, decorative pieces: just look at the classy offerings, from candle holders to cutlery, by the Danish silversmith Georg

Alvar Aalto's Savoy vase of 1936 is a classic piece of Finnish design, and has been produced in a wide range of colours and sizes.

Exposed brick and natural timber are a fine backdrop for Eames chairs and a PH Artichoke lamp (Poul Henningsen, 1958).

Mobiles are a frequently used decoration in Scandinavia. This striking model, the centrepiece of a traditional dining area, is in the style of American artist Alexander Calder (1898–1976), who influenced modern art throughout the world.

Keep clutter in check with masses of built-in storage, painted all-over white.

Jensen, at the range of timelessly beautiful Aalto vases or at the whimsical mobiles by the Danish company Flensted, made from the mid-1950s. To work well with the overall ethos, accessories should be elegant, spare and organic, and chosen with care so that they create maximum impact with minimum clutter. That's the secret of Scandi Sleek.

Mid-century Modern

Have fun with the light, bright
and cheerful look of fab and
funky 1950s style.

For die-hard fans of retro style, Mid-century Modern is *the* look to go for. The 1950s was the decade that changed everything, and that included design: the new 'contemporary style' was all the rage, and art, music, science and popular culture were its inspirations. For this look, the key ingredients are low, horizontal lines; sculptural but lightweight and practical shapes; bright, abstract patterns; and a certain sense of playfulness, optimism and informality.

Recognizable Mid-century Modern designer pieces are desirable, but certainly not essential. For this style, it is more about creating the spirit of the 1950s, and that resides in the likes of spindly-legged tables, chairs and sideboards, fabrics with patterns based on scientific forms or scribbly outline drawings, and lights that resemble hats or flying saucers. It's an appealing, streamlined look that can be either relatively low-key or

Left: Mid-century chairs and a typically bold abstract print make this an attractive corner.

Opposite: A sideboard is virtually essential in any mid-century scheme.

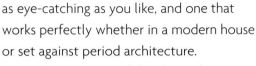
A selection of interesting furnishings is complemented by just the right choice of colour scheme.

as eye-catching as you like, and one that works perfectly whether in a modern house or set against period architecture.

Colours are crucial for the Mid-century Modern look. They are absolutely defining for this era, and everything will come together beautifully if you get them right: black and white, lemon-yellow, teal (a dark greenish-blue), tangerine, crimson, turquoise, acid green. Use this palette as your guide and you can't go wrong. Next, the basics: white walls or a natural grass-paper wallpaper would be fine, and ideal for a cool and restrained mid-century room. However, for a dash of authenticity, consider covering at least one wall in a wood-, stone- or marble-effect wallpaper, or one that has a pattern of trellis or lattice, atoms, space-age or scientific motifs, geometric abstracts (such as round-cornered squares or hourglass shapes) or starbursts.

In the kitchen, perhaps tile a splashback with images of fruit and vegetables, or of crockery, as produced by such British potteries as Beswick, Midwinter and Poole (see page 89). For the floor, patterned vinyl would be exciting, although maybe a little 'busy' for modern sensibilities; you might, instead, want

A stone-effect floor, conical lamp, sideboard and splay-legged chair make this an impressive retro room.

The Festival of Britain, 1951

The Festival of Britain introduced people to a new look in interior design, with lightweight furniture and bright, abstract patterns. The emblem on the poster was designed by Abram Games, one of the twentieth century's most respected graphic designers.

Organized to commemorate the centenary of the Great Exhibition of 1851, the Festival of Britain was a summer-long nationwide festival that celebrated Great Britain's contribution to civilization past, present and future, in the arts, science and industrial design. The focus of the Festival was an exhibition of buildings and pavilions on London's South Bank, including the futuristic Skylon and Dome of Discovery, as well as the newly built Royal Festival Hall. Among the highlights of the designs on show were Ernest Race's Antelope chair, made of a steel-rod frame with balled feet, and the Calyx fabric by Lucienne Day (see page 84). A landmark event, the Festival was, for many people, an introduction to modern design, and it wowed the 8.5 million visitors who came to have their spirits lifted after years of war and austerity.

A vintage coffee table makes the ideal centrepiece for a living room. Abstract patterns and glass accessories provide finishing touches.

to tone things down with a plain carpet, a wooden floor or a natural floor covering, with bright rugs scattered about to add comfort and define different areas.

The 1950s witnessed the development of many new materials. Make vinyl flooring, Formica and melamine part of your scheme (these are especially good in the kitchen) and you'll be re-creating that go-ahead, anything's-possible 1950s vibe. As for fabrics, along with wool, cotton and other natural materials, you should make use of what were then newly introduced man-made fibres, such as rayon,

nylon and Terylene. When making up soft furnishings, aim for slim upholstery, not deeply buttoned or frilled in any way, complemented by simple gathered curtains and, if you wish, a short fabric pelmet.

Furniture from the 1950s is fabulous fun; enjoy hunting out special pieces everywhere, from flea markets to second-hand shops, and from auctions to antiques dealers. Modern design of the times emphasized simplicity, with little or no surface decoration. This newly mass-produced furniture was slim, light and elegant, and was intended to look good

Opposite: Alvar Aalto designed his armchair no. 31 in the early 1930s. Here the seat is teamed with vintage fabric and a Sunburst clock (1950) by George Nelson.

Robin and Lucienne Day

Unlike their American contemporaries Charles and Ray Eames (see page 107), the British designers Robin and Lucienne Day tended to work independently rather than as a team, with Robin (1915–2010) designing low-cost, efficient and pared-down furniture, and Lucienne (1917–2010) creating dynamic, abstract printed textiles.

Robin's initial success came when he won a competition for low-cost furniture design held by the Museum of Modern Art, New York, in 1948, as a result of which he was appointed design director of the British manufacturer Hille in 1950. Over the next forty-five years he produced more than 150 furniture designs for the company, including the Q Stak bent plywood chair (1953) and the Polypropylene stacking chair (1963; below, right), which has sold millions around the globe.

In 1951 the couple were asked to contribute to the Festival of Britain (see page 81). Robin designed two room sets, and Lucienne created a furnishing fabric called Calyx, which featured a revolutionary abstract pattern inspired by plant forms (below, left). For decades her work – for Heal's, Liberty, Edinburgh Weavers and British Celanese – was hugely influential, and she also designed carpets, wallpaper, table linen and ceramics. Together, Robin and Lucienne Day transformed post-war British design.

Lucienne Day's Calyx fabric (1951) and Robin Day's Polypropylene stacking chairs (1963) were their most influential creations; together, the couple pioneered a new idiom in British design.

A vintage or repro print from the appropriate period creates instant (and inexpensive) retro style.

splayed legs, possibly even with bobble feet. Classic items are armchairs or side chairs, sofas, magazine racks, sideboards, cocktail cabinets, room dividers and occasional tables. Other typical shapes include artist's palettes, kidney beans and boomerangs, all ideal for coffee tables; you could also keep your eyes open for semicircular cocktail bars, and for coat racks featuring coloured plastic bobbles.

If you want to crank your style up a notch, consider investing in a designer piece around which you can base an entire scheme. The list of renowned designers from the period is

from all angles in open-plan rooms – when it wasn't built in, that is. Designers employed new materials and techniques that had been developed during the war, including laminated woods (especially plywood, solid wood being in short supply at the time), fibreglass, moulded plastics, cast aluminium and foam rubber (which replaced springs and horsehair in upholstery).

Seek out lean and low pieces, and if there's one rule to go by when buying Mid-century Modern furniture, it is always to include furniture with the period's typically spindly,

Choose a vintage desk with integrated storage for organized, stylish working, and then add some fun with retro toys, such as a miniature Eames elephant.

Left: For a fresh, modern take on retro style, choose a backdrop of plain white walls for your authentic furniture.

seemingly never-ending and includes the Brits Robin and Lucienne Day (see page 84) and Ernest Race; from the United States, Charles and Ray Eames (see page 107), Florence Knoll and George Nelson, Japanese-American Isamu Noguchi, Italian-born Harry Bertoia, and Finnish-born Eero Saarinen. Naturally, well-preserved original furnishings by such luminaries are only for those with deep pockets – but what an impact even a small piece would make.

Just as important as furniture for a Mid-century Modern style is the inclusion of some examples of the unmistakable light fittings that took 1950s homes by storm. A tidal wave of new designs washed away the old-fashioned examples that had prevailed; never before had so much choice been available, and in so many exciting materials and shapes. There is no shortage of 1950s lighting, sculptural and full of impact, to suit any room. The look could include anything from a bright-yellow woven-wicker shade in the shape of a coolie hat to an hourglass-like metal form, and from a plastic cone to an elegant white paper lantern. Other lights evoke mobile sculptures (the influence of

This G Plan teak-and-glass Astro coffee table dates from the 1960s, but looks great in a modern setting.

such artists as Alexander Calder and Piet Mondrian is obvious), or resemble rockets, flying saucers and pylons (science and the space age being all the rage at the time).

And now we come to the icing on the cake: mid-century accessories. Search out a streamlined, boldly coloured phone, a portable transistor radio, or a Ball wall clock in the manner of the much-imitated one designed by George Nelson in 1949 (see page 89). In the kitchen, brightly coloured, illustrated or labelled food canisters, utensils and gadgets would be great – just add a frilly

Stack retro ceramics and other accessories on shelves in the kitchen for a bright and cheery effect.

apron and you're done. For elsewhere in the home, you could choose any number of kitsch ornaments but, to keep it all in good taste, collectors may prefer to concentrate on British ceramics, Scandinavian and Italian glass, and British and Danish metalware.

Ceramics of the 1950s, by the likes of the British potteries Midwinter, Poole (see opposite), Meakin, Beswick, Ridgway and Carlton Ware, are instantly recognizable, with sometimes asymmetrical shapes and decorative patterns both abstract and representational, in graphic black and white or distinctive colours.

Designer glassware from Italy, combining traditional techniques with modern shapes and brilliant colours, is highly collectable, especially pieces by Paolo Venini, Ercole Barovier, Flavio Poli and Dino Martens. Glass designs from Finland and Sweden are equally accomplished, but more restrained in both colour and form; look for pieces designed for the Finnish manufacturer Iittala by Tapio Wirkkala and Timo Sarpaneva, or for the Swedish companies Orrefors and Kosta. Finally, keep an eye out for metal tableware by the British designers Robert Welch and

The mid-century pieces in this dining room have stood the test of time and still have huge appeal today.

The charming multicoloured
Ball clock was one of a series
designed by American
industrial designer George
Nelson between 1948 and 1960.

Poole Pottery's Freeform
range was hugely popular
when it was produced in
the 1950s, and still appeals
greatly to collectors today.
The pots shown here are in
the 'Bamboo' pattern.

David Mellor, and the Danes Henning Koppel
and Arne Jacobsen (see page 72); their
innovative, practical yet elegant and beautiful
teapots and coffee pots, jugs, toast racks,
candelabra and cutlery are just the thing
with which to adorn a Mid-century Modern
sideboard or dining table.

Poole Pottery

The Poole Pottery, founded in 1873 in Poole, Dorset,
started out producing tiles and architectural
ceramics. After the First World War, skilfully hand-
painted floral and Art Deco designs became the
company's signature, especially those by Truda Carter
(1890–1958), the pottery's chief designer in the 1920s.
The Second World War almost forced the factory to
close but, once restrictions on commercial pottery
manufacture were lifted in 1952, Poole soon capitalized
on the explosion in contemporary design, bringing
in new shapes, patterns and glazes. For almost a
decade the company produced a range of highly
collectable, cool, harmonious and handsome designs
in which abstract patterns are perfectly suited to
the flowing, 'freeform' shapes of the ceramics
themselves (below). The 1960s and 1970s, too,
were a great time for Poole, with the introduction
of such vividly coloured ranges
as Delphis and Aegean, also much
desired by collectors today.

Colourful Kitsch

It's a style that divides opinion, but there's no doubt that it adds exuberant colour and character.

Kitsch is one of those styles that you either love or hate. The term means different things to different people: for some, it's derogatory (dictionaries use such words as 'tawdry', 'tasteless', 'vulgar' and 'pretentious' to define it); for others, it's ironic; and for the style's fans it signifies a joyful celebration of unstuffy, everyday fun.

Whatever it means to us today, it was in the 1950s that kitsch really came into its own, although it wasn't called 'kitsch' at the time. After the dark, deprived war years, Europe and the United States exploded into a new tomorrow filled with bright colours, exciting patterns and crazy accessories. The buying public wanted more of everything, and couldn't have cared less whether it was deemed tasteful or not. People wanted new materials, new patterns and new labour-saving devices, and manufacturers were happy to

Depending on your preference, you can either limit your kitsch to an eye-catching corner display (left) or go for all-over colour, pattern and accessories (opposite).

Wacky Disney-character accessories (below) are just the things to add an element of kitsch to any room.

Plastic Fantastic

It's no exaggeration to say that plastic revolutionized the look of the 1950s. Housewives were offered a dream of low-maintenance, colourful kitchens, from vinyl flooring to laminated surfaces, complemented by unbreakable, mix-and-match melamine tableware, bright basket-weave chairs – and the ubiquitous pineapple-shaped ice bucket. But it wasn't all kitsch: in 1953 the American designer Russel Wright (1904–1976) launched his sober Residential melamine tableware range (below), designed to be used at the dining table as well as in the kitchen; it was given a Good Design Award by the Museum of Modern Art, New York. Plastic allowed people to leave behind forever the pre-war formality of porcelain and crystal, and was the domestic manifestation of a distinct change in society as a whole.

oblige. The market was soon bursting with frivolous items aimed at consumers with a taste for enhancing their homes. It was all about popular culture – and popular culture demanded kitsch.

If the high design and purism of Mid-century Modern (see page 78) aren't for you, there is plenty of retro style on offer in the form of Colourful Kitsch. But be aware: this is a look where a very little goes a long way, and although you may feel that your over-the-top decor is 'ironic', others may think you've got terrible taste. You have been warned. Strange

If you have amassed a collection of small things, a mantelpiece makes the ideal place for a display.

The colours of this sweet patterned Formica chair work very well with the table and black-and-white vinyl floor.

To introduce Colourful Kitsch into your home, take as your starting point a basic 1950s style: streamlined, lightweight and sculptural, all low, horizontal lines, slim upholstery and splayed, spindly legs. Your colour palette should be based on black and white, lemon-yellow, teal (a dark blue-green), tangerine, crimson, turquoise and acid green; some might say that the more the colours clash, the better. Add some boomerang-shaped coffee tables, a Formica-topped kitchen table with tubular metal legs and some idiosyncratic lighting – perhaps with

Don't be afraid to use rich colour and layers of pattern; the results can be glorious.

as it may sound, you could try for a 'tasteful' kitsch look by limiting your excesses to just one wall, shelf or corner of a room, blending them with a more restrained look elsewhere. Or you may decide that really isn't the point, and go the whole hog. Collectors may also be interested to note that some kitsch items, such as Formica units, limited-edition Barbie dolls and original lava lamps, are worth considering as an investment; although most objects were mass-produced and disposable, pieces that are rare, desirable and in good condition are increasing in value.

On open shelves and surfaces, pile up bright and breezy kitchenware for instant effect. Such items as those shown here are inexpensive and easy to collect.

The Green Lady

With her shiny black hair, scarlet lips and golden dress, the woman portrayed in the oil painting *Chinese Girl* (1950; shown below as a print) by the Russian artist Vladimir Tretchikoff would be classically beautiful, if it weren't for her mesmerizingly strange blue-green face. Tretchikoff (1913–2006) worked as a cartoonist in Shanghai and Singapore until the Second World War, after which he moved to Cape Town, South Africa, and began to exhibit highly coloured, romantic paintings of exotic women, to enormous, global success. Tretchikoff wanted to introduce art to the masses (and in doing so made himself fabulously rich), and, for working-class people, buying one of his prints was a way of bringing art, colour and life to their living-room walls. Critics may have hated it, but 'The Green Lady' is one of the most popular prints ever produced, and millions have been sold.

a brightly coloured, woven-plastic shade, or with a carved plaster base in the shape of a flamenco dancer. Now for the fun: the three main areas on which to concentrate are picking the perfect patterns, choosing kitsch for the walls and finding the right accessories.

Patterns of the 1950s are distinctive, and although some are relatively understated, a good many cross the line into what might be considered kitsch. Ceramics by the likes of the British potteries Midwinter and Beswick, for example, may feature novel shapes with 'artistic' patterns, ranging from subtle

For a subtle, pretty version of kitsch, choose colours and patterns carefully, and place them against a neutral background.

geometric or abstract shapes to scenes from the circus, poodles (we'll see more of those later), ballerinas, sketches of Continental streets and stylized plants. The same applies to wallpapers and fabric, which might also include imagery of cowboys (popularized by American television shows), African motifs, animal prints and surreal art.

In addition to wallpaper, walls may be adorned with all sorts of Colourful Kitsch hangings, prints and posters. Don't hold back: if you have always longed for a set of flying ducks (usually arranged as a group of three,

Even in a modern kitchen it is possible to create a kitsch effect, by showing off brightly coloured accessories on open shelving.

Left, below left and opposite, top: Children's toys make the basis of a lovely collection of kitsch objects.

Such ephemera as record sleeves, postcards and posters can add an appealing touch of colourful kitsch.

descending in size), now's your chance. Or you might prefer a disembodied head, carved in relief from plaster or ceramic; it could be a girl with a ponytail or an Asian lady, even a his-and-hers pair. Other wall ornaments were made of wire: perhaps a plant holder in the shape of a paint palette, or of a guitar. Alternatively, look out for prints of the sort of artwork that would probably make most critics wince but that was adored by the buying public. These works were often in lurid, technicolour hues, and either sentimental or exotic; one name to look

All-over pink creates girlie, fun and frivolous boudoir glamour.

Opposite: Ceramic ornaments, lamp bases and ashtrays can be the most kitsch items of all, especially when they are in the form of people or animals.

out for is Vladimir Tretchikoff, the self-taught painter of *Chinese Girl* (1950), dubbed 'The Green Lady' (see page 96).

The real make-or-break factor in the success of a Colourful Kitsch scheme comes from accessories. Nodding dogs and pineapple-shaped ice buckets must be top in the 'so bad they're good' stakes, closely followed by coloured-glass fish and clown bibelots, 'handkerchief' vases and ornaments in the shape of poodles or cats with elongated necks. The list of knick-knacks goes on and on: novelty cocktail glasses and shakers (in fact, novelty anything) and multicoloured drinks tumblers; ceramic figurines, ashtrays, trays and biscuit tins; clocks, telephones, radios and Teasmades; mirrors, magazine racks and plant holders ... Hugely enjoyable or hideous? It all depends on your point of view.

Right and far right, top and bottom: A hint of kitsch may be all you need to set the tone, as with this retro mug and radio, cute ornamental puppy and pineapple ice bucket.

American Dream

This bold, bright look includes some amazing designer furniture and the exuberant style of the American diner.

This appealing American retro style is all about being bigger and better, shinier and faster, more efficient and more streamlined. Chrome and leather, neon signs and car tail fins, huge refrigerators and glamorous furniture all characterize the look, which is colourful, upbeat, often larger than life and always appealingly confident.

The United States had emerged from the war years a rich and powerful nation, filled with energy and optimism. Pent-up consumer demand led to huge economic growth: gross national product doubled in the 1950s, and again in the 1960s. By 1960, the 'average' American family now owned a car, a fridge, a television and their own home. A housing boom, fuelled by affordable mortgages for returning servicemen, resulted in mile after mile of newly built prefabs. In this new suburbia, the modern (if basic)

A set of Eames DKR chairs, with pastel blue 'Bikini' pads, are a focal point in this American-style breakfast room, with rugged bare-brick walls and 1950s tableware.

This modern version of the 'dream kitchen' of the 1950s and 1960s features a sweep of units in man-made materials, a giant fridge and a Tulip table and chairs designed by Eero Saarinen in the mid-1950s.

Bold red is typical of the
mid-century American look,
whether in such accessories
as prints of Andy Warhol's
Campbell's soup tin (left) or
in furniture. Shown below is
the high-backed Bird lounge
chair designed by Harry
Bertoia in 1952.

open-plan homes all needed to be filled
with new furnishings, ready for the baby
boom that followed not long afterwards.
The kitchen was fast becoming the heart
of the home, and it was in America
that the idea of the 'dream kitchen' was
developed: a place in which doing the
cooking and washing up, the laundry and
ironing was not drudgery but supposedly
enjoyable, thanks to ranks of colourful
fitted cupboards with wipe-clean surfaces,
plus hordes of labour-saving devices and
handy gadgets.

From the natural grain of the wood panelling to the splayed-leg dining chairs (and even the palm tree in the corner), this dining area has all the elements of authentic American retro style.

Here, red leather and touches of chrome tie together the kitchen-bar and dining areas.

The new consumerism was fuelled by television advertising, but TV wasn't the only form of entertainment. This was the era of movie theatres, ice-cream parlours, coffee bars, dance halls, jazz clubs and the first shopping malls. People, especially the young, had money to spend and, whether it was on the latest tail-fin Cadillac or a new twin-tub washing machine, spend it they did. It wasn't long before what had once seemed like luxuries were considered to be necessities.

The United States was home to an up-and-coming generation of now legendary designers, many of them emerging from design and architecture schools at which the teachers were well-known European Modernists who had fled the Nazis a decade or so earlier. The talents of these designers, coupled with new technologies developed during the war years and inspired partnerships with forward-thinking manufacturers Knoll and Herman Miller, resulted in a golden age of American furniture.

To create the American Dream in your home today, concentrate on three areas: designer furniture; the drive-in or diner; and

The RAR rocking chair is part of the family of plastic chairs designed by Charles and Ray Eames in 1950. The collection also includes side chairs and armchairs on various bases.

Charles and Ray Eames

Husband and wife Charles and Ray Eames were the American powerhouse duo who changed the face of post-war design. They were architects, film-makers, toymakers and exhibition designers, but they are best known for their visionary furniture, which made innovative use of new materials and techniques. Charles (1907–1978) was an architect, Ray (1912–1988) an abstract artist; together they produced an extraordinary range of pieces, many of which are instantly recognizable as twentieth-century classics. Their big break came with a commission from the US Navy to design plywood splints; they later put their experience to use designing moulded-plywood furniture, and produced their first plywood chair in 1945. This was followed by the fibreglass RAR rocking chair in 1950 (below), and by wire chairs in 1951. Other celebrated designs include the Hang It All coat rack featuring multicoloured spheres (1953) and the luxurious leather-upholstered Lounge Chair of 1956 (see page 28).

Jukeboxes

Central to American popular culture, jukeboxes brought to life all kinds of music, from big bands to rock 'n' roll, during their heyday from the 1930s to the 1950s. Starting out as simple wooden boxes with coin slots and buttons, jukeboxes became ever more decorative, featuring beautiful timber veneers, satiny nickel plating, Art Deco styling with ziggurats, and masses of chrome. Later influences came from car design, with dashing lines and vivid lighting. Machines, by such companies as Rock-Ola, Ami, Seeburg and Wurlitzer, featured bubbles of gas moving through liquid-filled plastic tubes, domed tops, revolving cylinders, rainbow lighting and dramatic title displays (below). From the 1960s, the rise of the television heralded the slow demise of the jukebox as a vital source of entertainment; nevertheless, it remains a key symbol of American popular culture, and models are still to be found in diners, restaurants and clubs up and down the land.

the dream kitchen. Designer furniture is probably the trickiest. Charles and Ray Eames (see page 107), George Nelson, Florence Knoll, Harry Bertoia, Eero Saarinen and other mid-century American masters of modern furniture produced a series of what are now classic designs, and prices tend to be steep. If imitations don't bother you, they may be more affordable (just ensure that you are satisfied with the quality), while other, less famous designers produced work that may not be instantly recognizable but is, nevertheless, very much in the right style. Look for brightly coloured pieces made from fibreglass or plastic, or upholstered in nylon, with fluid and sculptural shapes. They will almost inevitably feature spindly, splayed, tubular metal legs; the exception being tables, chairs and footstools mounted on a central pedestal base.

As for the drive-in/diner influence, it's all about showy cars, fast food, the soda fountain and the jukebox (see left): jumping into your Caddy or Chevrolet for a cola with your friends, or hanging out at the drive-in watching *Rebel Without a Cause* (1955). For

In the early 1960s jukeboxes went space-age, with smooth button selectors and porthole-like 'bubble' tops covering the record changer.

A jukebox, neon lighting, a giant, Italian-language copy of a Campbell's soup tin and an innovative, sculptural chair: this room has all the elements of an American retro look.

Vintage wall art, such as these film posters, creates instant atmosphere in any retro scheme.

your home, think flamboyant, colourful, shiny and just a little bit kitsch: neon signs, diner-style seating (booths or chairs) in chrome and red leather or pastel plastic, black-and-white checked vinyl floors and food-related accessories, such as milkshake glasses or squeezy tomato-shaped sauce dispensers. Simply add a retro radio in plastic and chrome, its extravagant design inspired by car dashboards of the time.

This leads nicely to the idea of the dream kitchen, the fulfilment of every housewife's desires – or so the 1950s advertising would have us believe. Your dream kitchen should be fuss-free and easy to clean, thanks to a vinyl floor and patterned Formica surfaces, have loads of fitted cupboards for efficient storage and be dominated by a two-door fridge, preferably huge, pastel-coloured and chrome-trimmed.

You might want to heighten the cheerful atmosphere by fitting window curtains or blinds patterned with images of food and drink, and you should certainly consider featuring a few generously sized worktop appliances, in glorious colours combined with metal trims,

Chairs in American diners had to be both functional and attractive, and combined sturdy tubular metal legs with brightly coloured, well-padded leather seats and backs. Their classic design has stood the test of time.

Black-and-white flooring and neon strip lighting add character to this eye-catching kitchen. The 'quilting' on the metal splashback echoes the diamond pattern of the floor.

Left: Charles and Ray Eames designed the colourful Hang-It-All in 1953, and it has been hugely popular ever since.

Below, left: For instant American style, simply hang up a US flag.

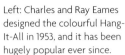

A vintage pinball machine and air pump bring a dash of retro fun to a modern home.

dynamic in shape and, in overall looks, obviously influenced by either space exploration or automobile styling. A toaster, kettle or food mixer is a good place to start, but don't forget juicers, blenders, waffle makers, irons, coffee makers and other gadgets. Some of these can be picked up for a song from a retro dealer, flea market or even car boot sale, but you'll find that others command surprisingly high prices, especially the more glamorous, eye-catching and substantial pieces. They are, after all, the epitome of the mid-century American dream.

The iconic Coca-Cola logo has become a universal symbol of American youth, exuberance and consumerism.

In the Groove

There's no holding back with this super, sexy and stylish look.

Fab, fun and funky, the style of the 1960s and early 1970s is all about attitude. It's a bright and bold look that is relatively easy to re-create, thanks to a proliferation of retro specialists operating on the internet, as well as dealers, auctions and second-hand shops. What's more, Groovy furnishings are often quite affordable, and because they are so eye-catching and exciting, you won't need very many of them in order to make an impact.

This was the era when Britain's post-war austerity truly ended; the world economy was thriving and, in a market dominated by youth, consumers had more options than ever before. It was a confident, optimistic time, with a strong sense of breaking away from the past and looking to the future, and the new 'popular' culture, inspired by comics, adverts, music, films and television, revelled in everything instant, frivolous and ephemeral.

You can keep things plain and still achieve a Groovy look, by inserting a few bold colours and adding iconic images.

Oversized letters spelling 'love' or 'peace' create a late 1960s/early 1970s vibe, especially when combined with colourful retro furniture and a 'Sputnik' chandelier, in which each arm extends to support a single light bulb.

Furniture from different eras can work well side by side: here the wooden sideboard is from the 1950s, but the shagpile rug and furniture with rounded corners have a 1960s feel.

Orange and yellow make for a totally Groovy (and very cheerful) room scheme.

Vivid colours and space-age silver, curvy plastic furniture in zany shapes, beanbags, shagpile carpets and the mind-boggling lava lamp (see page 122): all express the idea perfectly.

Clearly, this is not a look based on pale and pastel colours. Get into the Groovy mindset by using brilliant white paint as the backdrop for brightly coloured furniture and accessories. If that's not enough for you, consider painting one wall in metallic silver (painting all four in this way might create the feel of being inside a spaceship). Alternatively, try 1960s-style motifs, such as daisies, Union Jacks, bullseyes, rainbows, bubble lettering or swirling op-art patterns in black and white.

If freehand is not your thing, opt for original vintage wallpaper (find it on the internet), or a plain wall adorned with framed record sleeves of the era — many of them are works of art in their own right — or posters and

For an instant 1960s-style living space, insert a few pieces in space-age silver, some bright floor cushions and over-the-top wall art.

A transparent pedestal chair such as this is absolutely spot on for the Groovy style.

Vivid orange op-art walls and black Ant chairs by Arne Jacobsen are not for the faint-hearted, but if you love a bold look you will adore their powerful impact.

Werner Panton's plastic Panton chairs (1967) are sinuous and vibrant, especially in a dramatic shade of tomato-red.

digital prints. Artists to look out for include David Hockney, Roy Lichtenstein, Peter Blake and Andy Warhol, whose repeated, simplified images of Marilyn Monroe and Campbell's soup cans are icons of the era.

For the floor, all you need is neutral carpet, vinyl linoleum, timber or stone, although for die-hard Groovers there is nothing for it but to install silver floor tiles, primary-coloured carpet or wall-to-wall shagpile. And as for colours, well, as you've probably worked out by now, it's time to go bright, bright, bright, combining brilliant white with silver, red, yellow, blue, fluorescent orange, purple and apple-green.

For the Groovy style, subtlety is not at the top of your set of priorities. So in soft furnishings aim for instant impact rather than understated details. Fabrics might be of a single plain, dazzling colour, or patterned with large, graphic images or swirling op art. Look for synthetics, especially nylon, which was the big story of the 1960s; and bear in mind the importance of texture: rather than matt cottons and wools, choose fabrics that are shiny, stretchy, rubbery or plasticized. That man-made look is absolutely right for the period. Have curtains gathered on a simple track, and give fussy pelmets, edgings and tie-backs a miss. Upholstery should be tailored: no piping, frills or buttons. And bedlinen should be strong and sexy – black satin sheets, for example.

Verner Panton

Danish designer Verner Panton (1926–1998) was at the centre of the experimental, futuristic, exuberant 'pop' aesthetic in furniture and interiors of the 1960s. Having trained in architecture (where he was taught by the great lighting designer Poul Henningsen; see page 74), he first worked under Arne Jacobsen (see page 72), assisting on the design of the Ant chair. But he soon struck out on his own, becoming known for driving around Europe in a Volkswagen van that he had turned into a mobile studio.

Panton made his name as a visionary with the Cone chair of 1959 (below), which was followed by a design for the world's first inflatable seating. In 1965 the German company Thonet produced Panton's S chair, the first cantilever chair made of moulded plywood; but the designer will always be best known for another sexy and sleek cantilever chair, the Panton of 1967 (see opposite, bottom right), made from a single piece of coloured plastic.

Panton the man won numerous awards, and in addition to groundbreaking furniture he is renowned for his lighting designs (he had a long collaboration with the Danish lighting firm Louis Poulsen), textiles and 'far out' whole-room environments.

A corner of a living room to suit a Bond villain: black leather, chrome and a shagpile rug are the simple ingredients.

Below: The eye-catching Marshmallow sofa was designed by George Nelson in 1956, and remained a style icon through the 1960s. It could be described as one of the earliest Pop Art furniture designs.

The Groovy style has no time for formal, upright, classic furniture; instead, the emphasis is on flexible, low-cost, innovative pieces that emphasize informality. Their outlines should be bold and sculptural, and their colours confident. The style is summed up in the unconventional shapes produced by leading designers of the time (see opposite), but you don't have to spend a fortune on named designer furnishings; there are plenty of pieces available that emulate the look at reasonable prices, from modular furniture to stacking plastic chairs and beanbags. Even original G Plan pieces, which were produced from 1954 in High Wycombe, Buckinghamshire, by the E. Gomme company and hugely desirable at the time (especially its upmarket Danish Modern range of the early 1960s), are not terribly expensive to buy today. Get the essentials right and the rest will look after itself. A basic requirement is moulded plastic seating in dramatic, fluid outlines, with a touch of chrome and silver; look for straight legs (not splayed) or a central pedestal support, and choose stretch covers made of jersey or nylon.

Right: Moulded, over-the-top shapes are typical of furniture from the 1960s and early 1970s.

The Shape's the Thing

Iconic seating of the 1960s includes:

⊚ The spherical Ball, Bubble and Pastil chairs by the Finnish designer Eero Aarnio

⊚ The Cone, Heart Cone and S chairs by the Dane Verner Panton (see page 119)

⊚ From France, the Ribbon and Tongue chairs by Pierre Paulin, and Olivier Mourgue's Djinn seating (which appeared in Stanley Kubrick's sci-fi film of 1968, *2001: A Space Odyssey*)

⊚ The modular Tube seating system by the Italian Joe Colombo

⊚ Sofas in the shape of lips and baseball gloves

Flower power: patterns (here used on the rug and the lampshade) help to set the scene for a 1960s and 1970s style, and the shape of the lamp base is typical of the era.

Lava Lamps

Edward Craven Walker (1918–2000) was a great British inventor, entrepreneur and eccentric. The story goes that he was in a pub one night when he noticed a peculiar egg timer made from a cocktail shaker, old tins and some wax, and filled with liquid. Fascinated, he bought the contraption and decided to try to improve on its design. It took fifteen years, but in 1963 the Astro Lamp was launched by Craven Walker's company, Crestworth (the name was changed in 1992 to Mathmos). Dubbed 'lava lamp' after the waxy mixture that floated in the liquid as it was heated by the bulb, the lamp was an instant hit, appearing in TV shows including *The Prisoner*, *Doctor Who* and *The Avengers*. Lava lamps were made in a range of designs, and were ubiquitous until the late 1970s–early 1980s; they were revived in the 1990s and have since become wildly popular again.

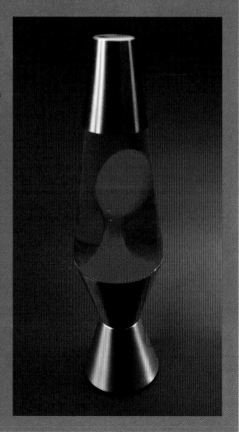

Lights can make or break a style, and you should regard them as being as important as a key chair, sofa or coffee table. The sexy plastic Panthella lamp (1971), a hemispherical shade on a slender stem with a flared base, by Verner Panton (see page 119), is an elegant example of designer style, as is the overarching Arco lamp (1962) by the Italian brothers Achille and Pier Giacomo Castiglioni, with its slab-like marble base and round metal shade (see photograph on pages 142–43); the latter is much imitated, so getting the look for a reasonable price is easy. There

Below and right: To add impact to your Groovy decor, choose plastic lights in sculptural shapes.

A table lamp with a base in the style of Verner Panton's Panthella lamp (1971) makes a great accessory. This purple is a wonderful colour, too.

Let science-fiction films from the 1960s influence your style: go for silver and transparent plastic, spherical shapes and pod-like seating.

A hanging chair was often the central feature of a Groovy pad of the 1960s and 1970s. The classic rattan version was created in 1957 by the Danish designer Nanna Ditzel, and its elongated pod-like form has since been much imitated (below); the Finn Eero Aarnio designed his acrylic hemispherical Bubble chair (right) in 1968.

are many other styles you could choose: fibre-optic or lava lamps (see page 122); Tiffany-style lamps with stained-glass shades; sculptural paper lanterns, as pioneered by the American–Japanese designer Isamu Noguchi in the 1950s; simple drum or cylinder shapes; spotlights; neon signs; and anything in the shape of a satellite, globe or flying saucer.

But the devil is in the detail, and when choosing Groovy accessories don't hold back for a minute: pick clocks and televisions in spherical, coloured-plastic casings, and add a plastic phone and a good-looking transistor

radio or hi-fi system (consumer electronics of the period by Braun and Bang & Olufsen are design icons). Houseware should include glass vases in saturated hues with elongated necks; bright melamine plates, bowls and cups; and ceramics with geometric prints. In particular, look for vintage pieces from the British potteries Denby, Hornsea, Meakin and Poole (see page 89), as examples of fashionable 1960s tableware.

Put it all together with panache, and the result will always be super, swinging, sexy and stylish.

Case

Studies

1 Living Room

The retro-style poster is a design by Frank Newbould, whose clients between the world wars included major British railway lines and London Transport.

Opposite: White-painted planked walls create a homely touch in this modern, high-ceilinged room, in which the colour palette is deliberately plain and simple. The light fittings are beautifully understated and utterly timeless in design.

Coastal Cool

There's a hint of Scandinavian mid-century style in this seaside bolthole.

The sensitive renovation of a 200-year-old stone cottage for contemporary living has created a simple but sparsely elegant seaside retreat, flooded with light and possessing a fab retro/modern feel.

This historic Scottish coastal home has been transformed by the addition of a green-oak and glass extension that features a vaulted ceiling, pale timber flooring and white-painted planking on the walls. There's a glorious sense of open, airy space, which is emphasized by the use of a limited colour palette: pure white with – appropriately enough for a coastal hideaway – splashes of clear blue and green.

In this super-cool living space, nothing could be more fitting than the comfortable mix of contemporary and retro furniture. The star of the show is undoubtedly the wooden Ercol Studio Couch, finished with elegantly slim cushions covered in a narrow-striped fabric. Its simple, slender shape cries out 1950s style, as do the typically splayed legs; these are echoed by those of the coffee table, another charming retro piece. Not all the period feel is from that era,

however: a great, local touch is the large reproduction of a railway poster, designed by the renowned British commercial artist Frank Newbould in the 1920s, advertising the beach at North Berwick. The flat, bright colours and stylized shapes so typical of his work are instantly recognizable.

Although the rest of the furniture is modern, it is unassuming and understated, slender and sleek, allowing the retro pieces to provide a focal point. Overall, the room feels fresh and bright – and rather Scandinavian. The key to Scandi retro style is an open-plan space that is full of light in summer but warm and cosy in winter; here, the wood-burning stove provides all the cosy-toes warmth you'd need. And mid-century Scandinavian design was all about natural blonde wood, used to make organically shaped furniture, combined with pale colours and slimline upholstery. It's a retro look that is as good-looking now as it was decades ago: simple, sculptural, natural and comfortable. Sit back, relax and enjoy.

Above: A wood-burning stove and retro wooden sofa give this room a Scandinavian feel. A huge sliding glass door leading directly on to the garden allows masses of light into the room.

Left: Slender, unfussy cushions are typical of sofas and armchairs from the 1950s.

2 Living Room

Home Comfort

Get cosy with the friendly warmth and charming good looks of this Nostalgia-infused living room.

If you're thinking of creating a Nostalgic retro style, for inspiration look no further than this welcoming living room. All the key ingredients are here. Let's start with the comfy brown leather armchairs — timeless classics that just look better and better the older they get. This mix-and-match pair (one has a wing back, the other hasn't) is given a homely touch with piles of colourful patterned and patchwork cushions; what's important here is the casual, pretty, thrown-together look. That effect is continued with the sofa cushions, another attractive mix of colours and styles in retro fabrics that add a cheery and informal character to the understated modern sofa.

Pattern and colour are key features of any retro style, and in this Victorian property they play counterpoint to the plainly painted walls and beautiful wooden floors. The eye is drawn by a crocheted throw, an armchair upholstered in fabric printed with tea roses and yet more roses painted on a wooden chest: the colours are bright and uplifting, the patterns heart-warmingly traditional in style. But there are also other, subtle features that underline the Nostalgic nature of this room: for example, the old wooden chest that's used

A pair of leather armchairs is comfortable and timeless in style. If you have upholstered furniture that has seen better days, cover it with a blanket or throw and pile on some pretty cushions. No one will notice.

You can't beat crochet for creating a sense of nostalgia. It's easy to learn, and is a great way to use up short lengths of different-coloured wool. If you can't face a big project, make small 'granny squares' and sew them together.

as a coffee table, and the wicker baskets that hold magazines and logs; the white china jug and the framed vintage prints; the floral lampshade and the lattice-work mirror frame. Even the frilled edging on some of the shelves contributes to the sense of traditional style, as does the soft blue paintwork on the cupboard doors.

Add a lovely selection of accessories, from a wooden-cased clock on the mantelpiece to decorated glass jars used to hold wild flowers, and you've got a delightful space that is bound to make you yearn for a taste of yesteryear.

Above: There are all sorts of ways to upcycle old furniture. Re-covering a chair in retro or contemporary fabric gives it a fantastic new lease of life.

Above, right: An informal display of flowers (real and crocheted) looks delightful in an array of glass receptacles.

Right: The colours in this variety of patterned cushions coordinate beautifully, and the bobble trims add a feminine touch.

3 Living Room

Light Fantastic

Furnishings from the 1950s blend happily with antiques and new pieces in this elegant Victorian home.

It is perfectly possible to achieve an appealing retro vibe with the lightest of touches, as is ably demonstrated in this eclectic living room. The space is flooded with light from a huge bay window and packed with original Victorian features, from the marble fireplaces and deep skirting boards to intricate cornices and elaborate ceiling roses. The owner, an eminent London florist, wanted to avoid an all-over period look, yet wasn't keen on overtly modern furniture, either. Instead, she opted for a good-looking mix of old and new.

Pages 134–35: Plain, off-white walls, timber flooring and a neutral rug provide a backdrop to an eclectic mix of pieces in this Victorian living room. An old industrial trolley provides a neat solution as a television stand.

Against a backdrop of off-white walls, honey-coloured oak flooring and shelves of books, the star of the show is, undoubtedly, the quirky 1950s coffee table, which features the splayed legs that are so typical of the era. With its panel of lime-green paint it makes a bright splash against the neutral-coloured, comfortable sofa, and is a great focal point in the centre of the room. By the window opposite, flanking an antique drop-leaf side table, are two retro armchairs, one from the 1950s (note the splayed legs again) and one older. They are full of character, but not

overtly idiosyncratic, and really suit the room: their simple modern upholstery picks up the greens and yellows used elsewhere, and they add an inviting retro elegance, rather than shouting 'look at me'. The woven cushion covers are modern, but add deliciously retro-style colour and pattern. All in all, the room shows that retro need not be overplayed or difficult, and that a subtle combination of pieces from different periods can really work well.

This fabulous 1950s coffee table creates a focal point in the room. Its lime-green panel coordinates beautifully with the bright cushions and yellow flowers.

Left: Accessories can contribute greatly to the feel of a room, and these elegant elongated glass candlesticks are definitely retro in style.

4 Living Room

Luxury with a Twist

In this city penthouse, glamorous Bauhaus style includes touches of humour and furnishings from a variety of eras.

Any interior designer will tell you that success is all about the details. The bigger picture is important, but if you fail to pay attention to the little things, such as light switches and door knobs, the overall effect will, in all probability, be slightly underwhelming. Naturally, in this penthouse apartment in Berlin – the second home of an interior designer – every last detail has been painstakingly thought through, from the colour of the doors and their frames (a dramatic black) to the arrangement of art on the walls.

Although the building dates back to the early twentieth century, this particular apartment suffered, when the present owner bought it several years ago, from a total lack of personality. It needed extensive remodelling, followed by an injection of decorative flair – and the starting point was to emulate the Bauhaus style that became

Page 137: There is nothing
like velvet – especially in
this beautiful soft grey –
for creating a feeling of
luxurious glamour.

Clockwise from top left:
The cocktail trolley is a
replica of one from the 1930s;
although this silver tea
service was made in England
in the nineteenth century, it
has a strong Art Deco look;
luscious surfaces are the
hallmark of the Luxe Moderne
look, and this sideboard has
an interesting rippled-metal
appearance; modern beaded
wall lights convey the
opulent style of the 1930s.

Right: A simple but sophisticated colour scheme sets off a range of soft textures in this superbly inviting living room.

Below: The dramatic clash of old and new can work very well, as demonstrated by the juxtaposition of these old oil paintings and a modern acrylic lamp by Ferrucio Laviani.

influential not long after the property was built. A revolutionary school of art, architecture and design that was established in Germany by the architect Walter Gropius in 1919, Bauhaus had a significant role in the development of Modernist architecture and design. In style it shunned ornamentation and favoured simple shapes and a harmony between form and function.

Here, the owner, who loves retro styles and enjoys mixing pieces from different sources to create personality and humour, decided to employ traditional, Bauhaus-like furniture, luxurious textures and a simple colour scheme based on pewter, putty and black – but with an added dose of retro fun, plus modern pieces and a few items sourced from travels around the world. A grey velvet sofa and two grey armchairs, all from Portugal, are placed with a pair of ornate beaten-metal coffee tables that were once Thai drums, and two antique table lamps with handmade modern shades. Near by is a transparent Bourgie table lamp (2004) by the Italian designer Ferrucio Laviani; it is nicely juxtaposed with inherited nineteenth-century oil paintings. Elsewhere, a very kitsch 1950s/'60s/'70s ethos is displayed in modern British lamps with bases in the form of various breeds of dog. This happy combination of pieces old and new is coherent yet retains an irreverent individuality.

5 Living Room

Inspired Eclectic

This airy apartment features
a scattering of key retro pieces ...
and a few surprises.

Given a bright and spacious period apartment
in a fashionable part of Glasgow, who could
resist incorporating some key pieces of
mid-twentieth-century designer cool?
Certainly not this owner (who is a designer
himself), although he has combined his retro

Opposite: The Polder sofa, designed by Hella Jongerius in 2005, complements perfectly the traditional wooden floor lamp in the corner of the room.

with modern design items, some high-street and junk-shop finds, and quite a few pieces that he made himself.

In the high-ceilinged sitting room, white walls and a polished timber floor provide a timeless backdrop for a dramatic sofa in shades of leafy green. Its blocky, horizontal form and muted colours are reminiscent of 1950s style, but in fact it was designed by the Dutch designer Hella Jongerius for Vitra in 2005. To one side is an E1027 side table by the Irish designer Eileen Gray, a classic dating from 1927, and by the window a junk-shop dining

Above: The American husband-and-wife team of Charles and Ray Eames designed the supremely comfortable Lounge Chair and matching ottoman as a gift for their friend, the film director Billy Wilder. It was first manufactured in 1956 by Herman Miller.

Left: Art Deco meets the 1980s in these colourful ceramics designed for the Rosenthal company by the American artist Dorothy Hafner.

table is matched with a set of plastic tub armchairs by Robin Day (see page 84), first launched in 1967. The star of the room, however, is the coffee table, made by the owner himself, inspired by the Italian designer Carlo Mollino, whose model 1114 table from about 1950 is similar, rare and very expensive.

In the study next door (above), the owner has also turned his hand to making the striking fire surround – a metal grid with concrete infill – and the side table, which employs zebrano wood and recycled 1950s legs. The wall piece (from Habitat) is striking, but the standout element is the lounger by Charles and Ray Eames (see page 107), a must-have on many a retro lover's list.

6 Living Room

Sixties Chic

This confident and comfortable living room offers a lesson in how to pull together a hip, happening retro look.

Retro is a great way to inject personality into a blank-canvas, modern home, and here the style is inspired by the swinging Sixties, the era of attitude, instant impact and fun, fun, fun. In this living room the eye is caught by the work that brightens up the wall, a colourful photographic piece with multiple digital images that brings to mind the work of Andy Warhol. The effect is heightened by the black framing, which makes the imagery stand out all the more. It's a strong, sexy look and it works brilliantly, the black contrasting dramatically with the white walls and toning with the grey sofas. The cushions, too, coordinate, and add a hint of op-art pattern reminiscent of the English artist Bridget Riley.

Flooring doesn't always figure very highly in the list of essentials for a retro room, but here an ivory-coloured shagpile rug is just the ticket: it almost screams '1960s', and is eye-catching but not ridiculously over the top (although not terribly practical if you have pets or children). Also distinctive is the fabulous arching lamp, as much a sculptural statement as it is illumination. It has been much imitated, but this is the real deal, an Arco lamp designed by Achille and Pier Giacomo Castiglioni for Flos in 1962.

The last word must go to the furniture. The simple, blocky and plainly coloured sofa and coffee table give the room a confident linearity. They contrast nicely

Warhol-esque wall art provides a dramatic focal point, as well as a jolt of colour in what is otherwise a largely monochromatic room.

with the mid-brown side chair, which, thanks to its angled outlines and buttoned upholstery, has more than a hint of Ludwig Mies van der Rohe's iconic Barcelona chair of 1929, or Florence Knoll's 1954 lounge seating. It's all comfortable and very good-looking: a retro/modern combination that works beautifully.

Bold lines contrast with the curving shape of the 1960s Arco lamp, and the side chair adds a strong retro feel. The shagpile rug provides a great textural effect.

The colours of this polished chunk of agate echo those of the furniture and cushions.

7 | Living Room

A Fine Vintage

Kitsch, colourful and quirky are the key themes in this home inspired by the 1960s and 1970s.

Lovers of retro design know that finding just the right piece depends on a variety of factors: research, legwork, persistence, patience and, quite often, a happy dose of luck. The internet has made life a lot easier, but it's still more tricky to get hold of the perfect retro piece than it is to visit a high-street shop and buy something new off the shelf.

Yet the results are well worth the effort involved, as can be seen in this eclectic retro home, which is bursting with quirky vintage finds wherever one looks. A terraced house in London, it has been fully renovated to

This happy mix of period details, modern sofas and retro items shows how attractive an eclectic mix can be.

Above: A fabulous shop mannequin such as this makes a striking kitsch ornament, but would also be useful for holding necklaces.

sideboard, alongside a collection of unusual accessories, from Christmas baubles to a neon shop sign. Other knockout pieces are the 1970s leather swivel chair and the unflashy 1960s G Plan Astro coffee table, in teak with a glass top. White walls provide a calm backdrop to all this busyness, but one wall is covered in floral wallpaper with a metallic sheen, the soft glitter of which echoes that of the mosaic mirror near by; further flourishes come in the form of Buddhas, peacock feathers, coloured glass vases and vintage toy cars. Last but not least, suitably 1970s in motivation are the framed typographic prints: 'Love' and 'Peace'.

uncover many original features, including gorgeous dark-wood floors, fine fireplaces and elaborate cornices. The owner has introduced an eclectic and colourful collection of mainly retro furnishings, sourced from a lifetime spent scouring flea markets and vintage shops, and picking things up on her travels.

It's hard to choose a standout piece among the furnishings and ornaments, but probably the most eye-catching of all is the green shop mannequin, which is just the sort of thing one longs to find on a retro-hunting trip. It sits proudly on top of a vintage

Children's clothes hanging on walls and doors as works of art are just as colourful and appealing as any painting.

Flea markets and vintage shops can yield some amazing finds, from a child's rocking chair to an old suitcase, and from colourful glassware to globes and alarm clocks.

A dash of metallic wallpaper adds glamour and intrigue, and looks fabulous as a backdrop to the groovy 1970s leather armchair.

8

Kitchen/Dining Room

Quality Counts

A limited colour palette and minimal styling serve to accentuate the allure of these classic twentieth-century designs.

The secret to using retro furniture is to go for quality; one or two well-made, classic designs will always look good, and have a much better chance of working well together than cheap pieces that won't stand the test of time.

There are no compromises in this stunning kitchen/diner. The owner has chosen a limited colour palette of black, white and brown, and minimally styled units, with just a splashback that features an intricate graphic pattern to lessen the room's severity. Even the floor is plain white, with the dramatic addition of a black hide rug; above this hangs a striking Copper

Shade light, launched in 2005 by the British designer Tom Dixon. These modern elements set the scene for some handsome furniture designed in the mid-twentieth century: a Tulip table (1956) by Eero Saarinen, and DSW chairs (1950) by Charles and Ray Eames (see page 107). Each design is iconic in its own right, yet as a group they work perfectly in their contemporary setting, thanks to their sculptural forms, which feature striking, simple lines. It's a great demonstration of how a considered use of retro items can be both elegantly functional and entirely up to date.

Above and opposite: The high ceilings of this kitchen/diner make the sculptural qualities of the furniture seem even more dramatic. The kitchen itself is minimal, as are the window treatments and the colour palette – the better to show off the carefully selected mid-century table and chairs.

9

Kitchen/Dining Room

Below, left: The shape of the enamelled-metal Semi pendant light (1967) is based on the arc of a quarter circle; the light's unique geometric form won it a design award from the Royal Danish Academy of Fine Arts.

Below: The Cherner armchair is an elegant classic of the late 1950s. Its designer, Norman Cherner, worked in many disciplines, from graphics, glassware and lighting to prefabricated houses and, of course, furniture.

Easy Elegance

Mid-century mingles with Arts and Crafts in this practical yet appealing dining room.

If ever one needed a reminder that the efforts and expense of building work are worth it in the end, this gorgeous house in Hampshire, southern England, would be it. Built in the 1930s, the property was utterly run-down when put up for sale, but the new owners were determined to bring it back to life as a family home. Taking a sensitive approach to the fabric of the building, they made essential repairs but, on the whole, retained the original, stylish and functional proportions and layout. Thankfully, plenty of original Arts and Crafts features remained, such as

Plain walls and a beautiful parquet floor provide a subtle backdrop for a collection of mid-century furnishings, bought by the owners over the years.

woodblock flooring, multi-paned windows and large fireplaces; their spare elegance provides a wonderful background for furniture, art and objects collected over the years.

Immediately striking is the architectural character of this unusual dining room: the oversized stone-and-tile fire surround, the warm wooden floor, the huge amount of light flooding in through rows of windows. The walls are a pale grey-blue, so that they are not too stark, and a range of modern artwork dominates one wall, thoughtfully hung so as to create a pleasing display.

To contrast with the Arts and Crafts architectural features, the furniture is mostly mid-century — sleek and strikingly good-looking. The yellow pendant lights are an award-winning design from 1967 called Semi, by the Danish architects Claus Bonderup and Torsten Thorup. The white chairs are the classic DSR by Charles and Ray Eames (see page 107), designed in 1948 (compare the metal legs with the wooden ones of the slightly later DSW, shown on pages 148 and 149). The *pièce de résistance* is the moulded plywood Cherner armchair with curved arms, as much a work of sculpture as it is furniture, designed by the American Norman Cherner in 1958. These items have been carefully chosen for their timeless and elegant looks, and complement the character of the house itself with sophistication, grace and understated flair.

10

Kitchen/Dining Room

An Eye for Colour

Retro and modern kitchen kit is displayed on open shelves for a look that's full of impact.

Left: In the hallway to the kitchen, the print of a young girl really sets the retro scene; hunt such gems out at car boot sales and in charity shops.

Above: Open shelves can be used to create attractive displays of even the most ordinary of everyday items.

Opposite: Vibrant colours set the scene in an informal room filled with cheery accessories.

If we all followed conventional wisdom, every small room would be painted white and furnished minimally; the idea is that this makes the space appear larger. But, thank goodness, not everyone plays by the rules; sometimes it's great fun to go for a splash of colour and an excess of kitsch, as in this charmingly chaotic bijou kitchen/diner.

The owner, a retro-inspired textile and homeware designer, painted the room a breezy blue and chose to show off lots of quirky, mismatching goodies rather than hide them away in cupboards. And bravo to her,

For practicality and a splash of cheerfulness, cover open kitchen shelves with wipeable sticky-backed plastic.

Textiles add character to any space, even the kitchen. Ironing-board covers, aprons and tea towels can all be interesting sources of pattern and colour.

because the apparently effortless combination of eclectic items creates a space in which one feels instantly relaxed and at home.

The intense blue is an ideal complement to the black-and-white vinyl floor (a classic for a retro kitchen) and plain, white-and-wood cupboards; it also happens to be a brilliant foil for the red Formica-topped table and brightly patterned accessories, including a red colander and an assortment of tumblers and mugs. There's no standing on ceremony here, and retro kit is muddled in with modern in a happy mix of the useful and the attractive. The finishing touches are a kitsch print of a young girl, by the doorway to the kitchen, and the 1960s-print tea towel thrown over the back of a chair – a real eye-catcher.

Kitchen/Dining Room

Black Magic

Alongside luxurious modern style, the owner of this sophisticated home has introduced a dash of retro character.

To demonstrate that retro furnishings can look amazing when teamed with avant-garde design, there is no better example than the dining room of this family home in Belgium, which dates back to the 1930s but has been remodelled by its interior-designer owner. The room is the epitome of contemporary chic, featuring a wide-planked wooden floor, dramatic contrasts of monochrome colour, superb lighting and an amazing feature wall. The style is very Luxe Moderne, redolent of sumptuous 1930s style, yet it has been achieved in a pared-down, modern way.

Low pendant shades over a dining table provide a pleasant light by which to eat; it's a clever idea to cluster different shapes at slightly varying heights.

A feature wall always adds interest to a room. Wallpaper is perfect, and easy to put up if you choose a wall without such features as radiators or doors; textured paint or a giant digital print are eye-catching alternatives.

Contemporary designer pieces include the white Container table by the Dutch designer Marcel Wanders, and the Beat family of beaten brass pendant lights by the British designer Tom Dixon. The stunning wallpaper is from the Pompeian range from Cole & Son; its 3D-effect geometry and colour combination are very Art Deco. Into this mix comes a set of modest chairs, of unknown origin but Scandi-retro in style, bought from a second-hand shop. Their black vinyl covering is perfect for the space; their timber framework introduces a pleasing note of natural beauty, and their modest style and vintage patina provide an ideal antidote to the sleek modern furnishings elsewhere in the room. The retro/second-hand theme is reiterated on smart white shelving through a display of objects that have been collected on the owner's travels or bought at antiques fairs and in second-hand shops. In their dark tones they fit the theme, but they also add interesting forms and textures, as well as a sense of history and a dash of more quirky character. Used in this way, retro has injected a friendly touch that makes the mix of objects in the room that much more delightful.

If you are planning to display a collection of disparate objects, try to choose a theme, whether it is shape, colour or texture. Here, the colour black pulls the look together; even the butterflies have been put into neat little black frames.

Kitchen/Dining Room

Pretty Perfect

Affordable appeal: a combination of simple old and new pieces with gorgeous patterns and dashes of vivid colour.

If ever there were an object lesson in the aesthetic benefits of combining vintage pieces with recycled items and a 'make do and mend' attitude, it would have to be this Victorian worker's cottage in Dorset, southern England. Its owner, the proprietor of a vintage-inspired shop, has decorated it with floral patterns, blue-and-white stripes, baskets, old-fashioned kitchen kit, knitting and crochet; it is delightfully pretty, and as cosy and comfortable as it's possible to be.

In the dining area, the lumpy, bumpy stone walls have simply been given a wash of white paint, all the better to show off a scalloped bevel-edged mirror (these have gone up in price in recent years, but are not impossibly expensive) and a retro-style traditional print. Its subject matter – pink and red roses – could hardly be more appropriate, and it coordinates perfectly

Opposite: A pretty tablecloth disguises even the cheapest of tables, and can be a focal point in itself.

with the tablecloth and chair cushion, the patterns of which are ideal for this Nostalgic look. Baskets tucked under the table provide useful and attractive storage, while the square-patterned cushion cover is divine – and just the sort of thing you could easily make yourself, using knitted or crocheted squares in coordinating colours.

Next door, in the kitchen, white-tiled walls are simplicity itself, complementing the planked ceiling and stone floor. If you are looking to put together an inexpensive but good-looking retro-style kitchen, this is a great

example. The key ingredients are a couple of white units with a wooden worktop, a plate rack, some bars with hanging hooks and a cupboard with glass doors. All work well to show off spotty and stripy mugs, traditional mixing bowls and all sorts of pots and pans. Dashes of bright red and blue provide jolly jolts of colour, as does the tablecloth with its retro-floral pattern. Overall, it's that perfect thing: a space where vintage, retro and modern blend seamlessly, and where good looks really haven't cost the earth.

Fitted kitchens may be modern and efficient, but an unfitted one looks charming and is usually less expensive to buy. What's more, you can incorporate retro elements, such as a glass-fronted cupboard (below, left) or a plate rack (below), in which to display your retro crockery and kitchen utensils.

13 Kitchen/Dining Room

Pale walls reflect the light that floods in from huge windows running the length of the room (just beyond the left-hand side of this photograph).

Dazzling Display

Designer furnishings complement vintage ceramics in this updated eighteenth-century home.

The ceramics displayed around the room were designed by some of the most important Italian pottery-makers of the twentieth century, and produced between 1928 and 1954 for Consortium of Italian Majolica Artists (CIMA). Both the late 1930s sideboard and the circular dining table were designed by Osvaldo Borsani, whose family firm, Atelier di Varedo, produced Art Deco-inspired furniture. In 1954, however, Borsani founded Tecno, which became known for its innovative designs.

The architect owner of this eighteenth-century house near Milan kept his renovated interior neutral and pale, with as few furnishings as possible, in order to show off both the furniture, bought from antiques markets over the years, and his prized collection of vividly coloured vintage ceramics.

This large room, probably once a barn or stable, now features utterly plain walls and a simple, warmly coloured, strip-wood floor. A pair of enormous Random lights by the Dutch designer Bertjan Pot for Moooi in 2002 float, moon-like, above the room, in which the main feature is a striking wooden sideboard with rounded ends and tapering legs, by the Italian designer Osvaldo Borsani. It was produced by Atelier di Varedo in about 1937, and today provides a perfect base for a display of mid-century maiolica ceramics by some of the major names in Italian pottery design, part of

a collection that has been put together by the owner over the course of more than twenty years. To add to the mix of decades, the round table (also designed by Borsani) dates from 1958, the Italian dining chairs (designer unknown) are from the 1970s, and the grey-upholstered fibreglass Rodica armchair is by Mario Brunu (1968). Overall, the colours are unified by the jewel-like highlights provided by the ceramics. Thanks to sleek and minimalist surfaces, and eye-catching but dignified furniture, the look radiates a sophisticated and authentic retro style.

14 Home Office

Home Works

A classic chair and retro accessories create a calm, comfortable and individual home office.

Introducing retro style to a home office may sound mad, but it has distinct advantages. A good new desk, for example, can be very expensive, but you'll probably find that a vintage desk is both well made and affordable. Or you could fit a simple wooden work surface along the length of a wall, as in this small but perfectly formed office, and complement it with narrow shelves supported by coordinating wooden brackets. As for lighting, there are many retro lamps around that would look wonderful on any home desk, and won't cost any more than a bland modern one. Hunt around junk shops, second-hand office-furniture stores and salvage yards for unique alternatives to conventional office furniture: old school lockers, a trestle resting on metal filing cabinets, a distressed kitchen unit or a desktop made from blackboard. Add an interesting chair (this is a DSW plastic chair, designed in 1950 by Charles and Ray Eames; see page 107), making sure that it's the right height for you to work at comfortably, and attractive accessories, from old wooden storage boxes to 1950s-fabric cushions, and you'll have an individual working environment that is the perfect place in which to be creative and productive.

Right, top: A row of vintage paperbacks can be decorative as well as a good read.

Right: Use a remnant of vintage fabric to make a cushion and create instant retro style.

White walls and a wooden floor: the calm simplicity of this home office is instantly appealing.

15 Home Office

Instant Impact

A single image is all that's needed to create wow factor in an informal home work area.

Whatever its style – from full-on working environment to a corner under the stairs – a home office needs to fit comfortably into the house as a whole, and even more so if it's on view all the time, or in a shared room where two functions must sit side by side.

This cute little space is not a proper home office (there's no storage, for a start), but it is one of those essential areas in which homework or letter-writing can be accomplished undisturbed, and is also a useful repository for drawing paper and pencils. A folding door ensures peace and quiet when required.

The office area flows seamlessly into the rest of the house, thanks to the use of the same cool grey flooring and clean white walls. The white Tulip chair (Eero Saarinen, 1956) makes a strong retro statement without being overpowering, while the wood-and-metal desk is elegant and simple. What draws the eye, of course, is the bold, bright print of Marilyn Monroe, first made by Pop artist Andy Warhol as a series of silkscreen images in the early 1960s. The print is a fabulous contrast to its understated surroundings and a great way to stamp personality on a functional space.

Folding doors are ideal for dividing spaces temporarily. This little work area can be screened off for privacy, or opened up to the light that pours in from the full-height glazing at the far end of the room.

Opposite: The sculptural form of the retro chair and the zingy colours of the 1960s print sing out against a clean, modern background.

16 Bathroom

Chequered Past

A black-and-white colour scheme gives this luxurious bathroom a strong retro vibe.

For dash and a debonair atmosphere, look no further than the Art Deco era. This bright and spacious bathroom in a Victorian terrace by the sea blends a taste of early twentieth-century retro style with twenty-first century efficiency. It all starts with a colour scheme: here, dramatic black and white, but either ivory or pistachio-green would also suit the look. Next, the surfaces – a white-painted wooden floor (inexpensive, practical and good-looking), white walls, and tiles laid in a traditional chequered pattern.

Now for the fittings. The large basin has that chunky, stepped shape so typical of the 1920s and 1930s, and the old-fashioned, cross-head taps are ideal. A plain, affordable modern bath has been boxed in attractively with tongue-and-groove boarding. And, rather than a concealed, contemporary style of shower, this exposed riser with an oversized rose is just the ticket, while the generously sized towel rail/heater complements it perfectly. Finally, accessories: the bevel-edged mirrors, glass shelves with chrome fixings and piles of fluffy towels create a sumptuous sanctuary of sophistication.

The stepped shape of this basin, together with its old-fashioned taps, is typical of the 1920s/1930s. Look for modern reproductions, or hunt out originals in salvage yards or online.

17 | Bathroom

Bathing Beauty

For a charming retro room, start with period details, add a traditional bath, and don't hold back on pretty accessories.

If you are lucky enough to own a home with original period features, decorating in a retro style will really help to make the most of them. This Victorian property boasts high ceilings, warmly patinated timber floors, intricate plasterwork, lovely sash windows, panelled doors and good fireplaces. And in this spacious bathroom all these gorgeous details are complemented by furniture and accessories in a charmingly Nostalgic retro look.

Claw-footed roll-top baths are ideal for re-creating a vintage vibe. If you're installing one for the first time, do check that your joists will take the combined weight of the bath (which is heavy), the water and the bather. This single-ended cast-iron bath is nicely placed against a shelf that holds useful toiletries and attractive accessories. The look is easy to replicate: simply collect some pressed glass and a few old floral saucers, enamelware tins or similar. Wrapped soaps are always a delight — you could even make your own packaging using remnants of wallpaper and some ribbon.

The other elements that make this room so sweet are the twirly wire shelf, the old-fashioned botanical prints, the large basket that doubles as a seat, and the painted free-standing bookshelf. All these items can be picked up inexpensively in markets, online or even at charity shops. Add some floral fabrics — slippers, dressing gowns and towels — and you have a room that's pretty as a picture and ready for relaxing in.

You can make an enormous difference to the overall appearance of a bathroom simply by changing the taps on a bath or basin. These antique brass bottle taps create a suitably Victorian look.

Opposite: Wood panelling painted in creamy tones is the perfect backdrop for a collection of traditional and pretty furnishings.

18 Bathroom

Shades of White

White tiles and retro fittings combine with modern touches to create a sophisticated sanctuary.

When considering room decoration, few people would deny that white is clean and calm, easy to live with, timeless and versatile. But if one looks carefully, this apparently all-white bathroom is actually a combination of white tiles (bevel-edged, laid in an offset, brick-bond pattern for a typically retro look), white-painted floorboards and cream-coloured walls. The subtle colour combination is less harsh than all-over pure white, and what makes it all the more attractive is the appealing combination of textures: glossy tiles, shiny glass, chalky walls and the softer surfaces of towels, sponges and brushes.

For a retro bathroom, the choice of sanitaryware is crucial, because it makes such a huge impact in the room. If possible, each piece should be on the large side, chunky even, with stepped or perhaps shell-like detailing. Finer touches here include exposed waste pipes and

Get the look with a wide basin in a stepped shape, cross-head taps and an exposed waste pipe.

Wall-mounting taps makes efficient use of space, and the right choice of fitting creates a strongly retro feel.

Textures are important when colours take a back seat: this mix of gloss and matt (below) is very attractive.

cross-headed taps for the basin, a wall-mounted cistern for the WC, and telephone-style shower head/taps for the bath. With the main furniture in place, add free-standing pieces – a stool, laundry basket or wall cupboard, for example – picked up from second-hand shops or markets and freshened up with a quick lick of paint. Here, a little side table has been given the treatment, and it's the ideal spot for a towel and some soaps. All in all, the room is light, bright and airy, and perfectly finished by the addition of a simple window blind and a potted plant – in white, of course.

Right: Don't be afraid to take a paintbrush to a small junk-shop piece; it can transform an unwanted item into a fantastic coordinating accessory.

19 Bedroom

Boudoir Bliss

Hints of colour and some retro furnishings make an elegant yet welcoming and relaxing room.

When one thinks about what one needs from a bedroom, it is less about space and practicality, and more about the room's emotional effect. Provided one has a comfortable bed, good storage and sufficient floor area in which to get dressed, the rest of the design preoccupations are likely to entail the putting together of textures, colours and lighting that make the space feel suitably welcoming and indulgent.

This sumptuous bedroom, in a period house in Edinburgh's New Town, has been refurbished for ultimate, boudoir-like luxury, and has more than a hint of Art Deco elegance. The first thing one notices is the combination of textures: soft woollen carpet, luscious on bare feet; a silky quilted bedcover; the tactile, suede-like finish of the chair's upholstery; the shimmery effect of the mother-of-pearl chandelier; reflective mirror

Opposite, top and bottom: Wallpaper with a subtle foliage pattern gives interest to a room without being overpowering. Add flair to a bedroom in the simplest way possible – with a good-looking bedcover and some decorative cushions.

Left, top and bottom: Make the most of any spare space in the bedroom with comfortable seating and a directional lamp. Mirrored furniture always has the glamour of Art Deco.

and barely-there glass. Then one takes in the colours: a clever mix of cream, beige and the natural tones of timber, with highlights of rusty red – just enough for warmth and individuality without being overpowering. The other key element is lighting, which in a bedroom must work as both bright, clear light for dressing, reading and putting on make-up, and softer, gentler light for relaxing. Here, the chandelier provides central light, but, as should be the case with all central pendant lights, it is supplemented by a variety of lamps: beside the bed, on the dressing table and, in the form of a marvellously sculptural multi-hinged floor lamp (reminiscent of the 1950s industrial lamps by the French company Jieldé), adjacent to the chair.

The mix of furniture is just as interesting. A traditional curly-metal bedstead is complemented by a classic painted wardrobe, a tower of hat boxes (useful as storage) and the eye-catching mirrored bedside and dressing tables, the latter in truly alluring 1930s style. The dressing table is a repository for pretty perfume bottles, compacts, jewellery boxes, vases and the like – an informal display that provides another decorative thrill and an opportunity for retro-loving collectors. Thanks in part to the hints of eclectic retro style, the room is perfectly planned, pretty without being cluttered, feminine without being frilly, and glamorous in an understated fashion.

20 Bedroom

Comfort and Joy

Soft colours, traditional furniture and pretty accessories add up to an informal mix in a room that is nicely Nostalgic.

Sometimes just one key item can make a room: its colour or pattern might inspire your entire decorative scheme, or it may have such strong, inherent character that other pieces need to coordinate with it, complement it or take a back seat to it. Sometimes, on the other hand, it isn't just one key item, but several; they may provide the backbone to a room, around which the other furnishings simply fit easily. So if you're stuck for ideas when decorating, this is a good way to start: take the essentials of the room (perhaps something practical or simply something you adore, such as a sofa or a vase) and build up from there.

For a retro bedroom such as this, in an 1880s terraced house in Gloucestershire, western England, the key pieces are the cast-iron bed and a dramatic red chaise longue (page 176). Both, like the house, are Victorian in style, and the rest of the room

An assortment of cushions makes this bed look appealingly cosy. This style depends on a choice of colours that coordinate, with contrasting plains, stripes, spots and flower patterns.

Below: Even if you don't use them regularly, old quilts and eiderdowns stacked in piles make charming decorative accessories.

The patination of a well-worn timber floor adds great character to a room.

takes its cue from this traditional look. The wooden chest of drawers and wardrobe are not trying to be anything other than what they are: simple, spacious storage that functions perfectly and sits well in the surroundings. One of the bedside tables is a painted wooden cabinet, probably made in the mid- to late twentieth century but timeless in style and just the sort of cheap, junk-shop find that anyone could renovate themselves using a bit of paint in a suitable colour. A huge mirror (it, too, timeless) looks fantastic propped against the wall, its ornate frame providing

a decorative counterpoint to the plain wall and the aged floorboards. An assortment of lamps ensures that the lighting is both flexible and attractive; scour second-hand shops and websites for just the right thing, and remember that they don't have to match. A floral blind and piles of plump pillows have cosy, comfortable, country-style charm. The finishing touches are retro-style accessories, including a playful little rocking horse, framed old prints and piles of gorgeous eiderdowns and quilts, perfectly Nostalgic bedding for a perfectly Nostalgic room.

A vintage treadle sewing machine makes a great side table, while a set of hooks is just right for storing and displaying necklaces.

Below: Re-cover sturdy old furniture to give it a new lease of life. Here, plain upholstery is partnered with a boldly patterned cushion.

21 Bedroom

Second-hand Style

A collection of furnishings found in flea markets and junk shops has been put together with subtle flair.

At the window, folding wooden shutters are simplicity itself, while a pale blind adds a touch of softness.

The limited colour palette ensures that disparate elements, such as a mid-twentieth-century chair and a traditional wardrobe, sit happily together.

The great thing about old furniture is that it is so environmentally friendly. By buying antique, vintage or second-hand, you are reusing precious resources and recycling (sometimes even upcycling) a lovely piece of furniture. Green issues aside, you will also be the proud owner of a small piece of history, an item that will probably be of high quality, reasonably priced and full of character. No wonder so many of us are getting into retro.

The owner of this period family home in Brighton, on the south coast of England, is an interiors stylist. She was buying and using retro furniture well before it became fashionable, and has furnished her entire house on a shoestring, mainly from car boot sales, flea markets, junk shops and second-hand outlets. This delightful bedroom manages to combine a feeling of cool serenity with an eclectic selection of interesting pieces. The most striking is the winged armchair and matching footstool, a Danish design inherited from the owner's grandmother and re-covered in linen. They complement a 1950s wooden Danish chair, a pine-topped table with painted legs, an early twentieth-century trunk and a modern curving bentwood stool. Simple floorboards and plain walls provide a subtle background; together with a limited colour palette of black, white and natural timber or leather, they ensure that the eclectic look works sublimely. Jewellery and other decorative pieces add a feminine touch to what is a pleasingly simple and entirely appealing space.

Delicate dresses provide decoration around the room. They are all Victorian, bought from flea markets in Brighton and London.

Left: The addition of something handmade brings unique warmth and character to a room. These papier mâché bowls are ideal for holding jewellery.

22 Bedroom

Modern Meets Mid-century

The sculptural lines of designer retro furniture stand out in this minimalist, monochrome room.

It comes as no surprise to find that the owners of this house – a renovated 1960s red-brick on England's south coast – are collectors of mid-twentieth-century furniture. Their supremely good-looking home, once a forlorn eyesore, is now a sleek and elegant luxury pad, containing some fabulous examples of classic design.

In this bedroom, a virtually all-white colour palette is balanced by the warmth of the honey-toned timber floor. The minimalist colour scheme allows the sculptural lines of the furniture to be shown to their best advantage. Quality counts, and it is better to keep the background calm and quiet. The chairs stand out immediately: a Swan chair designed in 1958 by Arne Jacobsen (see page 72), a Barcelona chair and footstool, designed by Ludwig Mies van der Rohe in 1929, and an RAR rocking chair, designed in 1950 by Charles and Ray Eames (see page 107). Even the bedside tables are Tulips, designed by Eero Saarinen in the mid-1950s. It is particularly lovely that the slender dressing table has a 1950s vibe, while the bed features a generously sized headboard with buttoned

upholstery that echoes that of the Barcelona chair. Everything is remarkably well considered, with complementary minimalist modern fittings, from the window blind and the tactile throw and cushions, to the black-and-white art and the display of glass bottles and gourds. The whole room works brilliantly because there is no clutter, allowing every beautifully proportioned piece to sit perfectly and confidently in its own place.

Opposite: Each element in the room is pared down and elegant, from the polished wooden floor to the plain, painted walls and simple window blind.

Right: This collection of glass bottles and gourds provides interesting outlines yet is suitably minimalist.

Below: Choose furniture on legs to make a room appear more spacious.

Directory

Nostalgic

Baileys
Whitecross Farm
Bridstow
Herefordshire HR9 6JU
UK
baileyshomeandgarden.com

A mix of vintage and new that's integral to a 'repair, reuse and rethink' philosophy

Betty Boyns
2 Tregenna Hill
St Ives
Cornwall TR26 1SE
UK
bettyboyns.co.uk

Fabric and homeware inspired by vintage, retro and country themes

Cath Kidston
cathkidston.co.uk

Witty, colourful and classic English style

GreenGate
int.greengate.dk for branches

Nostalgic and pretty patterned homewares

Labour & Wait
85 Redchurch Street
London E2 7DJ
UK
labourandwait.co.uk

Timeless, functional products for everyday life

Melin Tregwynt
Castlemorris
Haverfordwest
Pembrokeshire SA62 5UX
UK
melintregwynt.co.uk

Traditional Welsh weaving combined with innovative modern design

Toast
toast.co.uk

Linens, crockery and accessories with a relaxed look

Designer classics

Aram
110 Drury Lane
London WC2B 5SG
UK
aram.co.uk

Modern furniture, lighting and accessories, plus new work by young designers

Artek
artek.fi

Scandinavian specialist, with pieces by Alvar Aalto, Eero Aarnio and Tapio Wirkkala, among others

The Conran Shop
conranshop.co.uk

Furniture, lighting, accessories and gifts

Fritz Hansen
fritzhansen.com

Danish specialist, with classic furniture by Arne Jacobsen, Hans Wegner, Poul Kjaerholm and others

Geoffrey Drayton
85 Hampstead Road
London NW1 2PL
UK
and
104 High Street
Epping
Essex CM16 4AF
UK
geoffrey-drayton.co.uk

Furniture and lighting from Europe's leading designers and manufacturers

Herman Miller
hermanmiller.com

Classic pieces by Charles and Ray Eames and George Nelson from their original collaborator

Hive
820 NW Glisan Street
Portland, OR 97209
USA
http://hivemodern.com

Authorized retailer for Alessi, Artemide, Artifort, Carl Hansen & Co., Cassina, Flos, Kartell, Knoll and Vitra, among others

Knoll
knoll.com

Signature design pieces by the likes of Florence Knoll, Eero Saarinen and Harry Bertoia

Louis Poulsen
louispoulsen.com

Lighting by Verner Panton, Arne Jacobsen, Poul Henningsen and others

SCP
135 Curtain Road
London EC2A 3BX
UK
and
87 Westbourne Grove
London W2 4UL
UK
scp.co.uk

Classic and new furnishings that are functional, beautiful and made to last

Selfridges
selfridges.com

Stylish department store with great homeware

Skandium
245–249 Brompton Road
London SW3 2EP
UK
and
86 Marylebone High Street
London W1U 4QS
UK
skandium.com

A wide range of Scandinavian brands

Vitra
vitra.com

A wide range of classic furnishings by renowned designers

Vintage

After Noah
121 Upper Street
London N1 1QP
UK
afternoah.com

Unusual and interesting antique, vintage and contemporary furnishings

Antikmodern
antikmodern.blogspot.com

Mid-century modern and vintage furniture and accessories

B&T Antiques
47 Ledbury Road
London W11 2AA
UK
bntantiques.co.uk

Signature mirrored pieces and other stylish twentieth-century antiques

Baxter & Liebchen
33 Jay Street
(corner of Plymouth Street)
Brooklyn, NY 11201
USA
baxterliebchen.com

A carefully selected range of furnishings, from Danish Mid-century Modern to 1970s pop

Dad-Design
dad-design.co.uk

A wide selection of original mid-twentieth-century furniture and homeware

Dansk Møbelkunst Gallery
Aldersrogade 6C
2100 Copenhagen
Denmark
and
53 bis quai des Grands Augustins
75006 Paris
France
and

Talacker 30
8001 Zürich
Switzerland
dmk.dk

A leading authority on Danish design from the 1920s to the 1970s, especially rare Modernist furniture and lighting

Decennia Design
Meelstraat 82
5025KN Tilburg
The Netherlands
decenniadesign.nl

Twentieth-century furnishings, collectables, accessories and lighting at affordable prices

Decoratum
31–33 Church Street
London NW8 8ES
UK
decoratum.com

High-quality twentieth-century and contemporary design

Elephant & Monkey
35 Killigrew Street
Falmouth
Cornwall TR11 3PW
UK
elephantandmonkey.co.uk

Classic, mid-century British furniture, and upcycled chairs and sofas in contemporary fabrics

Elliott & Tate
55 Dalston Lane
London E8 2NG
UK
elliottandtate.com

High-quality vintage Danish furniture

Fragile
fragiledesign.com

Original mid-twentieth-century furniture and homeware

Histoire
Turfstraat 7a
6811 HL Arnhem
The Netherlands
histoire.nl

High-quality designer furniture, special lighting and vintage objects with a history

Judith Michael & Daughter
73 Regents Park Road
London NW1 8UY
UK
judithmichael.com

Brimming with antique and vintage treasures

Kirkmodern
Sandymount
Dublin 4
Ireland
kirkmodern.com

A range of original mid-century decorative items and design, especially Scandinavian and British

Lost City Arts
18 Cooper Square
New York, NY 10003
USA
lostcityarts.com

A leading source of twentieth-century designer furniture, lighting and accessories

Lovely & Company
lovelyandcompany.co.uk

A personal selection of 'modern vintage'

Made-Good
made-good.com

Post-war furniture and collectables

Mark Frisman
527 Warren Street
Hudson, NY 12534
USA
markfrisman.com

High-quality twentieth-century designer furnishings

Mark Parrish Mid Century Modern
Unit 17
Cirencester Business Estate
Elliott Road
Cirencester
Gloucestershire GL7 1YS
UK
markparrish.co.uk

Familiar and not-so-familiar household objects and artefacts from the mid-twentieth century

The Modern Warehouse
(by appointment)
3 Trafalgar Mews
London E9 5JG
UK
themodernwarehouse.com

Vintage mid-century furniture with a focus on Scandinavian, American and British design

Nanadobbie
16 Gloucester Road
North Laines
Brighton BN1 4AD
UK
and
8 Fore Street
Lostwithiel
Cornwall PL22 0BP
UK
nanadobbie.com

Vintage, retro and industrial wares; specializes in Scandinavian glass and ceramics, as well as affordable furniture

Orange and Brown
121 St Georges Road
Bristol BS1 5UW
UK
orangeandbrown.co.uk

Classic mid-century furniture

OurShowHome
ourshowhome.com

Design that looks good and works practically in the home, and has done for half a century

Pineapple Ice Bucket
Lyndhurst Road
Brockenhurst
Hampshire SO42 7RH
UK
pineappleicebucket.co.uk

Vintage homeware, fashion and accessories

Pink Flamingos
pink-flamingos.co.uk

American designers from the twentieth century

Pure Imagination
(by appointment)
2 Westoe Village
South Shields
Tyne and Wear NE33 3DZ
UK
vintageretro.co.uk

Vintage Scandinavian and English furniture, design, decorative objects, lighting and accessories

Retro Bazaar
68 Alston Drive
Bradwell Abbey
Milton Keynes
Buckinghamshire MK13 9HB
UK
retro-bazaar.co.uk

Telephones, clocks, lights, record players and radios restored to their former glory

Retropolitan
retropolitan.co.uk

Stylish and affordable decorative vintage homeware

Retrowow
retrowow.co.uk

An online source of information about the period from the 1950s to the 1980s

Roomscape
(by appointment)
in the CityStore
Belmont Street
London NW1 8FH
UK
roomscape.net

Specializes in high-quality and affordable vintage furniture, lighting and decorative arts

Sputnik Modern
1901 North Henderson Avenue
Dallas, TX 75206
USA
sputnikmodern.com

High-quality twentieth-century furniture and lighting

Tuderhoff
tuderhoff.com

Vintage pieces from the twentieth century, including mid-century Scandinavian, Art Deco and great industrial finds

Twentieth Century Antiques
twentiethcenturyantiques.co.uk

Modernist, mid-century and post-war design

Twentieth Century Interiors
twentiethcenturyinteriors.com

Mid-century furniture, fabrics, lighting and glass

TwentyTwentyOne
274 Upper Street
London N1 2UA
UK
and
18C River Street
London EC1R 1XN
UK
twentytwentyone.com

Furniture, lighting and accessories by inspirational twentieth- and twenty-first-century designers

Winter's Moon
wintersmoon.co.uk

A quirky assortment of vintage, recycled or handmade furniture and home accessories

Zwischenzeit
Raumerstr. 35
10437 Berlin
Germany
zwischenzeit.org

Design classics and everyday pieces from the 1950s to the 1970s

Modern Vintage

Crown
crownpaint.co.uk

The Vintage range of flat matt emulsion colours reflects popular culture from the 1940s to the 1980s

Emma Loves Retro
emmalovesretro.co.uk

Cushions and home accessories, handmade in the United Kingdom

Fired Earth
firedearth.com

Paint colours that capture the spirit of the 1950s

Jane Foster Designs
janefoster.co.uk for stockists

Fabric and screen-prints inspired by the 1960s

Little Greene
littlegreene.com

The Retrospectives paint collection offers colours from the 1960s and 1970s

Mini Moderns
minimoderns.com

Wallpaper, textiles and home accessories with a retro/modern style

New Retro Dining
newretrodining.com

Custom-made 1950s-style dining furniture from the USA

Acknowledgements

A big thank you to the talented team at Merrell for always being so supportive and lovely to work with. I should also like to thank my husband, Martin, for his quiet encouragement, and to dedicate this book, with my love, to Felix, Tegan and Orlando.

Picture Credits

© Nick Dunmur/Alamy: 122(l).

GAP Interiors/Graham Atkins-Hughes: Jacket, back(tr); 9(t), 15, 37, 38 (designer: Serrano Evans), 83, 96(l), 101(bl), 137, 138(tl), 138(tr), 138(bl), 138(br), 139(tr), 139(br), 150(l), 150(r), 151(l), 189.

GAP Interiors/Devis Bionaz: 7(r), 66, 67, 69(t), 69(bl), 69(br), 74(l), 97(r).

GAP Interiors/Mark Bolton: 46(r), 108, 116(l).

GAP Interiors/Johnny Bouchier: 9(b), 22(r), 42, 114, 124, 125(b).

GAP Interiors/BUILT: 110(b), 111, 120(b).

GAP Interiors/Nick Carter: Jacket, back(tl); 8(t), 25, 43, 45, 46(l), 47(l), 47(r), 49(r), 50, 57, 62(b), 63(b), 64(l), 64(r), 98(bl), 158, 159(l), 159(r).

GAP Interiors/Bieke Claessens: 56(r), 74(r; designer: Luc Debuyser), 142–43, 144(l), 144(r), 155, 156–57, 157, 164, 165.

GAP Interiors/David Cleveland: Jacket, back(cl); 61 (SHH Architects), 162(t), 162(b), 163.

GAP Interiors/Dan Duchars: 35, 44(l), 49(l), 53(b), 60(tr), 70, 90, 93, 100(br), 101(br), 145(l), 145(r), 146(l), 146(r), 147, 152(l), 152(r), 153, 154(l), 154(r).

GAP Interiors/Cristina Fiorentini: 14(t), 16, 36, 160, 161(t), 161(b).

GAP Interiors/Jake Fitzjones: 48, 59(b).

GAP Interiors/Piotr Gesicki: 59(t), 82.

GAP Interiors/Douglas Gibb: 1, 4, 7(l), 27, 28, 30, 31(t), 51, 54, 56(l), 60(br), 62(t), 63(tr), 77(l), 86(b), 97(l), 104, 120(t), 125(t), 128, 129, 130(t), 130(b), 140, 141(l), 141 (r), 172(t), 172(b), 173(t), 173(b).

GAP Interiors/Tria Giovan – Stern & Bucek: 102–103, 106(t).

GAP Interiors/Glow Decor: 39.

GAP Interiors/Bruce Hemming: 26, 91, 92(r), 166–67.

GAP Interiors/House&Leisure: 87(r).

GAP Interiors/House&Leisure/K. Bernstein (architect: J. Jacobson): 113.

GAP Interiors/House&Leisure/J. de Villiers: 99(r), 118(l), 123(l).

GAP Interiors/House&Leisure/DOOK: 80(t).

GAP Interiors/House&Leisure/M. Green: 123(tr).

GAP Interiors/House&Leisure/M. Hall: 23.

GAP Interiors/House&Leisure/Warren Heath (stylist: Julia Stadler): 53(t), 68(b), 98(tl), 99(l).

GAP Interiors/House&Leisure/Micky Hoyle: 8(b), 12 (styling: Tracy Lee Lynch), 65(r).

GAP Interiors/House&Leisure/S. Inggs: 58.

GAP Interiors/House&Leisure/D. Ross: 29.

GAP Interiors/House&Leisure/M. Williams: 110(t), 122(r).

GAP Interiors/Alexander James: 86(t), 116(r), 118(tr).

GAP Interiors/Patric Johansson: 73(r), 75(l; design: Alvar Aalto), 148, 149.

GAP Interiors/Bill Kingston: Jacket, front; 31(b), 79, 89(l), 112(bl), 115.

GAP Interiors/Benjamin Mamet: 6, 78, 80(b), 88, 96(r), 106(b; architect: Pierre Bragnier).

GAP Interiors/Clive Nichols: 55.

GAP Interiors/Clive Nichols – Kally Ellis: 134–35, 136(l), 136(r).

GAP Interiors/Mark Nicholson: 100(tl), 105(r).

GAP Interiors/Costas Picadas: Jacket, back(bl; designer: Peter Lam); jacket, back (br); 17, 18, 24, 32, 60(l), 65(l; designer: Peter Lam), 73(l), 85(l), 85(r), 101(t), 105(l), 107, 109, 112(tl), 112(r), 117, 118(br), 119, 121, 182.

GAP Interiors/Spike Powell: 63(tl).

GAP Interiors/Mark Scott: 20–21, 22(l), 52, 75(r), 77(r).

GAP Interiors/Rachael Smith: 14(b), 44(r), 68(t), 76, 87(l), 94(t), 98(r), 123(br).

GAP Interiors/Robin Stubbert: Jacket, back(cr); 19 (architect: Wayne Swadron), 33, 34, 71.

GAP Interiors/Amanda Turner: 131, 132, 133(l), 133(tr), 133(br), 168, 169, 174, 175(l), 175(r), 176(t), 176(b).

GAP Interiors/Rachel Whiting: 13, 72(l; styling: Francine Kay), 72(r; styling: Francine Kay), 94(b), 95, 170(t), 170(b), 171(t), 171(b), 177, 178, 179(t), 179(b), 180 (styling: Francine Kay), 181(t; styling: Francine Kay), 181(b; styling: Francine Kay).

GAP Interiors/Mel Yates (design: Abigail Ahern): 100(tr), 100(bl).

© MASCA, courtesy of Manitoga/The Russel Wright Design Center: 92(l).

© SliceofLondonLife/Alamy: 81(l).

© John Smart/pooleimages.co.uk: 89r.

© Amoret Tanner/Alamy: 81(r).

© V&A Images/Alamy: 84(l), 84(r).

Index

First published 2012 by
Merrell Publishers, London and New York

Merrell Publishers Limited
81 Southwark Street
London SE1 0HX

merrellpublishers.com

British Library Cataloguing-in-Publication Data:
Sorrell, Katherine.
Retro home.
1. Interior decoration. 2. Retro (Style)
I. Title
747-dc23

ISBN 978-1-8589-4581-1

Produced by Merrell Publishers Limited
Designed by Nicola Bailey
Project-managed by Marion Moisy
Indexed by Hilary Bird

Printed and bound in China

Jacket, front
Sideboard from the 1950s

Jacket, back
Left to right, top to bottom: see pages 25, 96, 163, 71, 65,
and 182

Page 1
Sideboard from the 1950s, leather armchair with a 1930s
style, and Bestlite floor lamp (1930) by Robert Dudley Best

Page 4
Tulip table (mid-1950s) by Eero Saarinen, and Panton chairs
(1967) by Werner Panton (see page 119)

Page 182
Bubble chair (1968) by Eero Aarnio

Page 191
Loge armchair and stool (1989) by Gerard van den Berg